Praise for WATERCOLORS

The rescue of JJ the whale symbolizes the potential power that humans possess to protect our oceans, reduce our impact on the planet, and prevent harmful consequences from climate change. Terry Tamminen's latest book, *Watercolors*, is a call to action to once and for all save our oceans.

—Robert F. Kennedy, Jr.,
President, Waterkeeper Alliance,
and environmental activist

In *Watercolors*, Terry reminds us of the magic, originality, and beauty Mother Nature provides. He inspires us to take action ourselves to protect and preserve the wonders of our planet.

—Ed Begley, Jr.,
actor, environmental activist,
and author of *Ed Begley, Jr.'s Guide to Sustainable Living*

Tamminen's book was an enjoyable, educational, and inspirational read. It is evident that he possesses a true admiration for the ocean and its inhabitants, and as a reader it's impossible not to feel that as well.

—Beau Bridges,
actor and environmental activist

Global climate change is the challenge of our time. JJ the whale is a reminder of the urgency behind this challenge, and why we must curb greenhouse gas emissions and create a clean energy economy.

—Michael Northrop,
Program Director, Rockefeller Brothers Foundation

The way Terry tells this touching story about the rescue of a baby gray whale moved me deeply. Eloquently expressed and beautifully interwoven with entertaining characters and his first hand experiences, Terry clearly conveys that whether it is the rescue of one precious baby whale, or our precious planet, we must all work together. I know that the people who read this beautiful story will be as inspired as I was.

—Bonnie Reiss,
environmentalist and former California Secretary of Education

The inspiring story of JJ the whale moves us to ponder issues bigger than the rescue of a single whale. JJ ultimately surfaces as a symbol for the desperate need to preserve and protect Earth's sacred oceans. Read *Watercolors*. It is a compelling true story with profound implications for Planet Water.

—Captain Charles Moore,
Founder of Algalita Marine Research Foundation
and author of *Plastic Ocean*

Tamminen tells an emotional and captivating story that reflects the beauty and frailty of the ocean. We are impacting our oceans in ways that we can't yet see and certainly don't completely understand. Tamminen reminds us that unless we take action now to support our ocean's health, "JJs" will soon cease to exist.

—Anne Earhart,
environmentalist, Founder and President of the Marisla Foundation

About WATERCOLORS

What would you do if you found an abandoned baby, who was hungry and confused? What would you do if this baby was a whale?

Terry Tamminen, former Secretary of the California Environmental Protection Agency, shares his remarkable true story about the rescue of JJ the whale, a day old gray whale that was found abandoned in Marina del Rey, California. He takes us through his incredible journey and the setbacks he encountered, including bureaucratic obstacles, the daunting task of figuring out what and how to feed a 1600 pound baby, and finding a safe home for the infant.

Not only is this a book about whale rescue, but a touching example of human will and compassion. Tamminen introduces us to the various characters involved—many volunteering their time to save the animal, all deeply devoted to saving the animal—creating an emotional picture of the power of human collaboration.

Compelling and riveting, Watercolors captures the urgency felt by the people involved in the rescue. At the same time, it educates the reader about gray whales, providing a glimpse into their life experiences. But most importantly, this book is a call to action: although we may not all have the chance encounter of meeting and directly saving a baby whale, our actions and decisions that we make on a daily basis are affecting these mysteriously beautiful creatures.

WATERCOLORS: HOW JJ THE WHALE SAVED US

First published in 2011 by

SEVENTH GENERATION ADVISORS

in the United States of America

Seventh Generation Advisors,
2601 Ocean Park Blvd., Suite 311, Santa Monica, CA 90405.

ISBN-13: 978-0615553955 (Custom Universal)
ISBN-10: 0615553958

Library of Congress Control Number: 2011918680

Design by Rob Siders, 52novels.com

First Edition: November 2011

Watercolors

HOW JJ THE WHALE SAVED US

A true story by
Terry Tamminen

7th GENERATION
Advisors

www.seventhgenerationadvisors.org
www.watercolorsthebook.com

To the hundreds of hands who saved a baby whale—
like watercolors on canvas, yours is a story that is beautiful, but not
easily defined, illuminating and concealing the truth that lies beneath.

Acknowledgments

This entire book is an acknowledgment of those who lived, and therefore wrote, the story of a whale named JJ, but as always there are unsung heroes.

First, allow me to thank the tireless campaigners who work for community organizations large and small, trying to push back the tide of assaults on our oceans. But you and I can offer more than gratitude—100% of the profits from the sale of this book will support these non-profits and the people who give so much. Thank you for your contribution by buying this book and please consider asking others to do likewise for a very good cause and for what I hope will be an entertaining and enlightening journey in the reading of it.

Most copies of Watercolors will be sold as e-books, a relatively new way to share stories. Having worked with great publishers on my books in several genres in the past, I hesitated to move to a more entrepreneurial format, but must thank Jenna Cittadino for helping me understand publishing in the 21ST Century and for helping me take the leap. Kris Haddad, who was with me at the Santa Monica BayKeeper and features prominently in Watercolors, was also instrumental in helping to get this book into print. My appreciation and thanks to them both.

I would not have served as the Santa Monica BayKeeper and been on the water that eventful day in January 1997 without the faith and encouragement of Dan Emmett, Luanne and Frank Wells, Rob Wells, Paul Heeschen, Gil Segel, Richard Baskin, Lisette and Norman Ackerberg, Ruby Raitt Evans, Beto Bedolfe, Robb Rice, and Rick Luskin. Thanks to you all for seeing the plight of our ocean planet and refusing to stand by and let it happen unchallenged.

Fast forward through quite a few years and battle scars, today I have the privilege to work with an amazingly talented and dedicated team at Seventh Generation Advisors. In addition to Kris and Jenna, thanks to Andria Mack, Sasha Abelson, and Jill Gravender. They believe, as I do, that no matter how daunting the challenges, we will prevail and we are not alone.

Finally, my wife Leslie Tamminen has been more than a supporter of this project. She is one of the most determined advocates for eliminating plastic pollution from the ocean, a topic that deserves a book of its own (and I hope she will one day write it!). Together, we know that whales like JJ will not live out their normal lifespan if the human inhabitants fail to change the course of ocean destruction that is accelerating our own tenuous grasp of a quality life on this planet. My hope is that more people and policymakers will heed Leslie's call to action, saving far more than whales in the process.

Table of Contents

Photos and Illustrations

Chapter 1

OF CREATURES GREAT AND GREATER

Sunrise. Santa Monica beach. Warm, golden, shiny in summer. Biting, metallic, misty in winter. Either way, Beverly Hoskinson and her Boston terrier "Bucky" walked along the shoreline every morning, sharing it with musclemen, tourists, joggers, seashell hunters, plastic trash, bums, tai chi practitioners, lifeguards, evangelists, kelp mounds, sand flies, and skittish sandpipers.

This particular mid-winter morning was damp and downright gloomy, as Beverly stretched methodically on a rock jetty, preparing for her daily exercise and, perhaps, for a modicum of motivation to face another eight hours in the office cubicle. As the director of a large foundation, her job was one that brought joy to many others—she gave money away to good causes. It was, however, tethered to a desk, a commute, a smart business suit and practical shoes, and, like most jobs, a routine. Perhaps that is why Beverly Hoskinson would consider January 11, 1997, one of the most memorable days of her life. It was anything but routine.

"BayKeeper Hotline, this is Terry," I said, my standard response when the citizen tipster phone rang at my desk on the houseboat that served as an office.

"Hi, it's Bev Hoskinson. I know we're supposed to meet later today, but I want to report a whale now."

"Uh, OK," I mumbled hesitantly. As the "aquacop" for the coastal waters of Los Angeles, I was used to getting tips on pollution or poaching in the Santa Monica Bay at all hours, but wasn't sure why Beverly was calling about a whale. I might have been a bit intimidated by the fact that she was planning to visit the BayKeeper headquarters later that morning to consider our small non-profit organization for a grant. It seemed like some sort of test.

"Well, I mean a baby whale, rolling around in the surf here outside the breakwater," she continued. "I was on the north jetty and heard a strange sound like rushing air. Couldn't imagine what it was. I looked down through the darkness and spotted what appears to be a small whale."

"You sure it's not a big box or something?" I regretted doubting her the moment the words were spoken. I just essentially called her an idiot and could visualize my grant drifting out to sea.

"No," she said with practiced patience and a touch of good humor. "It's a whale."

A few days earlier in a heavy rain, our staff scientist had video-taped a refrigerator floating down Ballona Creek, along with tons of other trash and debris, discharging with billions of gallons of polluted stormwater from Los Angeles city streets out to the coastal waters near the marina. Had she spotted the errant fridge, I wondered, but thankfully, not aloud. I suggested she meet me at my patrol boat and we would investigate together. Even if it was an inanimate object, doing the grant interview while patrolling the local waters looking for Beverly's whale was a better bet than sitting in the office.

I hung up the phone, grabbed a jacket and my super-sized coffee mug, then crossed the dock to the patrol boat. A cool, grey fog had taken up permanent residence as the first full morning light streaked across the waters of Marina del Rey. A lone fishing boat ploughed through the main channel past the silent gasoline dock on its way out to Palos Verdes. The night shift of the Sheriff's Harbor Patrol collected their gear from boat Bravo and scurried up the gangway to the warmth and bright incandescent light of the station. Two pelicans dive-bombed a school of anchovies near the guest docks. The smell of coffee wafted faintly from one or two boats of the six thousand in "The World's Largest Man-Made Recreational Boat Harbor" as live-aboards awoke and prepared to assault, or be assaulted, by another big-city day. The peculiar early-morning theatre of the marina routine had begun. Boaters clad in terry cloth shuffled up to rest room and shower facilities on dry land, carrying steaming mugs, towels, and toothbrushes.

On the dock near the patrol boat a great blue heron extended to its full height and squawked a prehistoric croak-croak-croak, registering disgust that the fish it had been following had darted beneath a boat and out of sight. The magnificent night hunter spread its wings and with several laconic slaps was airborne, drifting across the still waters. This night's work was over.

If Beverly had seen a whale, what would it be? Blue whales, the largest creatures ever to roam the earth, cruised through southern California waters at times, but certainly not to give birth to their calves. Killer whales are more frequent visitors, but more on par with tourists than residents, who might use the bay as a maternity ward. Gray whales are a common sight offshore, but their annual migration brings them southbound in fall and northbound in spring, so a rare sight in January. A floating kitchen appliance was more likely than any of them.

More to the point, what would we do with a baby whale if we found one? Darwin would say let it perish. A generation weaned on imagery from Cousteau, Disney, and Greenpeace might say it must be rescued at all cost. In between lay a calculus that would argue, considering the damage we've done to whales and their habitat, we should help every one of them to survive—but you can't take a half-ton baby home in a shoebox and feed it from an eye dropper.

So why couldn't it be a whale? Those days seemed filled with all manner of contradictions, oddities, and enigmas. It was 1997, the Year of the Ox—there are no sea animals in the Chinese zodiac, despite the fact that ours is an ocean planet. President Bill Clinton was about to be inaugurated for his second term, preparing to deal with many of the same leaders in Congress who had forced a government shutdown down two years earlier in a stalemate over the federal budget. In the twelve months prior, the IBM computer "Deep Blue" beat chess champion Gary Kasparov for the first time. Canadian singer Alanis Morissette became the youngest person ever to win a "best album" Grammy and *Braveheart*, with an Australian actor in a movie about Scotland made by Americans, took best picture at the Oscars.

Survival was a theme that year and not just for a baby whale in a California marina. In the worst climbing season on record, twelve died on Mt. Everest, but one Swede rode his bike to Nepal and made the ascent successfully without oxygen. The Hoover Institution, a conservative think tank in California, released a report claiming that global warming would provide Americans with "valuable benefits." Perhaps Hoover-ites had become "irrationally exuberant" (a phrase applied by Federal Reserve Chairman Alan Greenspan that year to the stock market) by GM's release of the EV1, an electric car the Detroit automaker later destroyed, along with the hopes of many who were eager to end our oil addiction. Mad cow disease struck England while Princess Diana and Prince Charles were divorced. OJ Simpson stood trial for murder.

Michael Jordan and his Chicago Bulls had won another NBA title, just months before Atlanta hosted the Summer Olympic Games. NASA discovered primitive life on a meteorite thought to originate from Mars, while an obscure primitive on earth, Osama bin Laden, wrote an essay calling for "jihad on the Americans" for "occupying" Saudi Arabia. Mother Teresa was awarded honorary US citizenship, although it wasn't clear she ever asked for it.

In Los Angeles, immigrants battled for recognition and rights, as a ballot measure sought to deprive them of both, while *Escape From LA* played at cineplexes. The UN tussled with Iraq over inspections, no-fly zones, and various other hostilities, but the Dow Jones Industrial Average closed above 6,000 for the first time in history.

Thinking back on those days and these innumerable strange events, a baby whale lost among fiberglass hulks of an urban harbor didn't seem so implausible.

As the sun rose higher behind its soft gray shroud, Beverly and Kris Haddad, my thirty-something second in command at the BayKeeper, boarded the patrol boat with me. I navigated out of the protected waters of Marina del Rey, past rowboats and celebrity mega-yachts alike, and on towards the open ocean near Venice and Santa Monica beaches. An elegant woman in her fifties, Beverly shivered in her brightly colored jogging suit as the open boat sliced through waves and mist. Kris handed her a blanket and I zipped up the vest around my chunky middle-aged frame as we chatted about our work and hers. Kris was a northern California native and loved this soupy, cold, foggy weather. I am solar-powered, but prefer any day on the ocean to one indoors, regardless of weather.

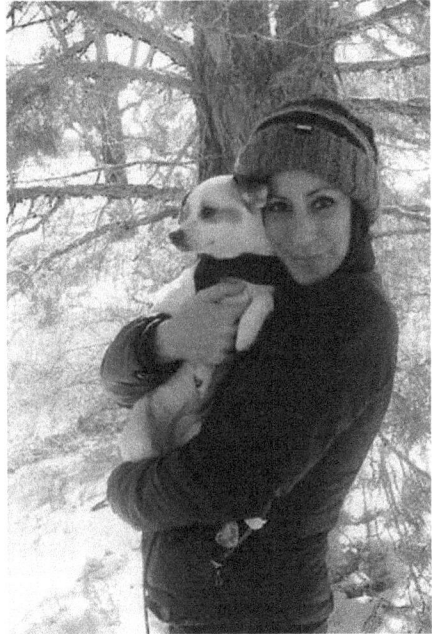

Figure 1a: *Kristina Haddad*

"What's that?" Beverly asked, pointing just past the break-water in the general direction of the beach. I turned the boat slightly to follow her outstretched arm like following the needle on a compass and, when both aligned, I too saw a dark box-like object, mostly sub-merged, bobbing in the gentle surf about a hundred yards ahead.

Fog clung to the ocean, turning to rivulets of moisture running down our cheeks and dripping from the brim of my cap. The object disappeared behind each swell, lost in gray on gray. Creeping forward to avoid hitting anything, the picture came into focus slower than a 1997 dial-up Internet connection. As we halved the distance to the target, the "fridge" showed a tail and slid beneath the surface.

A number of ocean creatures leave tracks in the water when they dive, flattened ovals of gently rippling water in the middle of the otherwise jumbled wind waves, breakers, and salty foam. Sea lions, rays, marlin, dolphins, and whales. The track in front of us, almost as large as the boat itself, would have been evidence enough of a living sea animal, but the tail left no doubt we had just seen a small gray whale.

Figure 1b: *Beverly Hoskinson*

Although a baby gray whale in the Santa Monica Bay would be rare, the middle of January is indeed their average birth date, but normally an event reserved for the warm lagoons of Baja several hundred miles to the south. Its conception would have been about four hundred days earlier. He/she would have already migrated in-utero more than twelve thousand miles since then, from Mexico to the Arctic and back, becoming an embryo that more resembled a bird than a marine mammal, starting life with a rounded head, a beak, and small winglets that would one day become stabilizing pectoral fins and a more familiar whale's shape.

"Maybe that was a tail," Beverly suggested hesitatingly. As her words dissolved into the steady vibrations of the motor, we felt something bump rudely into the side of the boat and instantly saw the other end of a whale.

Rolling and rising like a log pushed beneath the surface that refuses to stay submerged, about six feet of gray rubbery skin emerged, punctuated only by two slits that serve as nostrils on the top of a head. A gray whale calf parted the waters, much of its true length and bulk still hidden beneath the waves, bouncing against the right side of the boat. She rotated slightly, raising her left side out of the water, an action necessitated because her natural line-of-sight, her world, lay below, not above. An iridescent black eye stared up at my brown one and waited for something to happen.

"Beverly, there's your whale," I proclaimed, faking a tone of knew-it-all-along. We each blurted out oh-my-gods and this-is-amazings as we leaned over the starboard side of the boat and stroked a creature that few ever see and fewer ever touch.

"I think she likes this," Kris guessed. "Where do you suppose the mother is?"

"In this fog, she could be twenty feet away," I suggested, suddenly realizing that the mother may not like us so close to her baby.

Figure 2: *Our first sighting of JJ*

As the thrill of interspecies communication gave way to practical concerns, it also occurred to me that this baby must need a lot of milk. Despite a few very obvious differences, gray whales are a lot like us. Air breathing, warm-blooded mammals, live birth, suckle their young, live to seventy years or so. Newborns instinctively press against two slits on either side of the mother's considerable underbelly, stimulating nipples to emerge. With no real lips to form suction, nursing is not easy, facilitated instead by the baby's supple, massive tongue and by the mother's muscles that pump rich, yellow, half-and-half (at fifty percent fat, whale milk is ten times richer than a human's). When the baby loses its grip, streams of milk can spurt five feet into the air like an errant fire hose, but the calories that do make it through are essential to the early health of a newborn.

"She may be hungry," I wondered aloud. "Depending on where the mother is, she may not have eaten in awhile."

Slowly, two parts of this odd picture began to draw into focus. First, this calf thought the patrol boat was its mother, nuzzling the side and bottom looking for a nipple. Second, this calf would not survive unless we could reunite it with its mother.

"How do you know if it's a he or a she?" Beverly asked.

"Genitals are hidden in a body cavity," I recalled from a lecture on a whale-watching trip. "Won't be any easy way to find out. One thing we had better figure out fast though, is where is the mother?"

Let us assume this particular infant is a female, as we later learned was true. Let us call her JJ, the name SeaWorld later gave her, honoring a volunteer marine biologist recently deceased. Even at birth, a gray whale is too large to hug—this "infant" was already close to three quarters of a ton and about fourteen feet long. So why is it that when you look into one of JJ's shimmery, inky eyes, you wrap your heart around hers in an instant? What bonds a creature to humans, inspires us to care for it when that creature seems so alien in form and function?

The Bible suggests that whales have always been benighted above all others—"and God created great whales, and every living creature that moveth, which the waters brought forth abundantly…and God

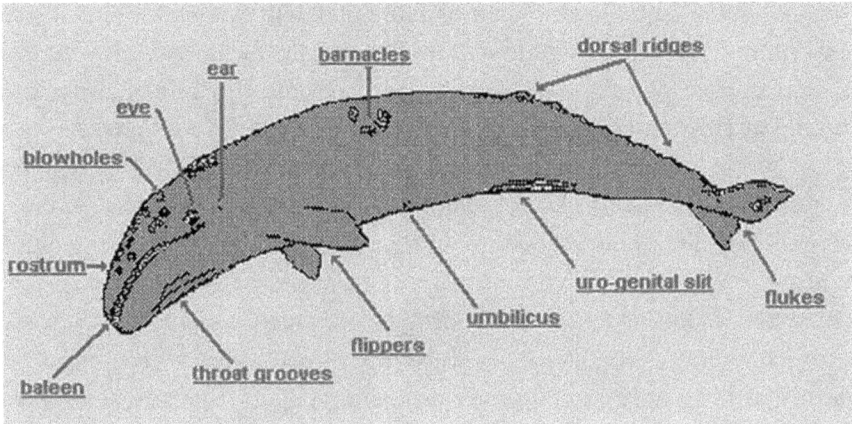

Figure 3: *Gray whale features*

saw that it was good." Whale ancestors date back sixty million years and originally sported four legs and a tail, likely evolving to sea creatures by wading into water for food and holding their breath to feed. Some evolved into hippos, some evolved into whales, slowly losing hair and gaining a more streamlined body that concealed teats and genitals. Forelimbs flattened over time into flukes that still contain hand and finger bones today; the hind limbs and pelvis disappeared leaving small bony remnants embedded in side muscles, becoming a tail built like an aircraft wing for maximum propulsion efficiency.

When something is perfectly suited to its environment, it doesn't change much thereafter. Gray whale bones of a hundred thousand years ago are virtually identical to those of today, making it one of the most ancient creatures on earth, far older than modern humans. Despite whales and humans sharing the planet for so long and despite both being mammals, our relationship was mostly one of ignorance and, therefore, fear. Romans dubbed whales "sea monsters" and centuries later Herman Melville described Jonah being swallowed by a whale "seething into the yawning jaws awaiting him, all his ivory teeth, like so many white bolts upon his prison."

But long before car bumpers bore stickers defending whales or kids were taught to cry "Free Willy," some cultures knew that whales were not so alien. Thirteen-hundred year old cave carvings in India depict the god Vishnu in the form of half man, half whale, an early sense of comradeship not shared with other animals. Gray whales were depicted in cave paintings in Mexico that pre-date the 1400s, about the time that English common law declared the whale "a royal fish."

Noble or common, monster or martyr, the whale has always given our species reason to marvel. The largest of them, blue whales, have arteries that are greater in diameter than the water pipes of large cities and pulse with such force that beats can be heard two miles away. Lay three school buses end to end; bring three more alongside; stack six more atop those first six; fill each of the dozen buses with a hundred adults and you approximate their size and weight—the largest animals ever to exist on earth, yet able to migrate thousands of miles a year or dive to two miles below the surface for hours at a time.

"Sometimes the whale shakes its tremendous tail in the air, which, cracking like a whip, resounds to the distance of three or four miles," Melville reports in Moby Dick. Using more than a tale to make noise, some whales are known to stun giant squid with blasts of sound from drums of oil in their great skulls, but their true power may lie in more subtle attributes, such as the unique cells in the whale's skin that excrete lubricants to make it smoother/faster in its liquid environment or their highly developed taste buds that compensate for a lack of smell. Perhaps most wondrous is that whales, like the grays and blues, attain their gargantuan stature by feeding primarily on some of the tiniest creatures in the sea, the diminutive shrimp-like krill, consuming the equivalent of three thousand double-double cheeseburgers with bacon every day.

Beverly shifted her focus from the waterline to the distant shore, one moment visible through breaks in the fog and the next moment vanishing like Brigadoon. She saw dozens of people milling about near the water's edge, no more than two hundred yards away, talking animatedly and pointing in our general direction. The shifting mist also revealed one of the Los Angeles Sheriff's lifeguard boats, moving slowly toward us.

Shelly Butler, the "Baywatch" chief, hollered out that they had been trying to keep boaters from accidentally hitting the whale since first spotting it on the beach some hours earlier. They had called Peter Wallerstein of the Whale Rescue Team to help them push her back into the water. Shelly said Peter had reported the remnants of an umbilical cord, confirming it was a newborn, but no one had seen other whales nearby. In this fog, finding the mother, even a whale-sized mother, would be needle-in-a-watery-haystack stuff.

A few months before JJ swam into our lives, Hillary Rodham Clinton published *It Takes a Village,* a book about the many hands and hearts needed to make successful adults out of our children. As I watched Kris and Beverly speaking to JJ and trying to understand her movements; the lifeguards in their boats and on the beach standing ready to assist, but without a clue about what to do; and passersby gathering on the rocky jetties straining for a glimpse through relentless fog, it was becoming obvious that this child's future would be largely dependent upon a multi-faceted village too.

By mid-morning, as the "village" grew larger, Beverly reluctantly acknowledged that she would have to get to her office at some point today. Kris would need to handle phones and radios back at our HQ, where more calls were likely coming from press and the public. When JJ swam off towards the Sheriff's boat, I slowly backed off and turned the patrol boat in towards the marina.

Motoring back to the dock, it seemed that Beverly hadn't exhaled since we first sighted JJ, but now settled back onto the seat forward of the helm station. She spoke animatedly, recounting every detail of the encounter, much like a teenager after shaking hands with a rock star. Beverly was born in Liberal, Kansas, a town she noted was about as far from "liberal" as you can get, but equally far away from the ocean and any chance to see a whale up close. She may have gained her love of the sea from her heritage, which includes great grandfather Drake, a descendant of the famed English mariner Sir Francis Drake. Sir Francis sailed the California coastal waters several hundred years earlier, making maps of previously uncharted waters. Beverly talked about being good at a few things in life, chief among them was her sense of direction, much like her famous ancestor.

Otherwise, Beverly's family was comprised of wheat farmers, ranchers, carpenters, oil field workers, teachers and merchants, all generally enjoying a happy and prosperous life until the Dust Bowl and depression turned the world around in the 1930s, nothing suggesting a connection to the sea. Her parents moved to Colorado in 1942, where she grew up in a suburb of Denver. Her father dabbled in politics and the family enjoyed summers in the Rockies—perhaps the shaping forces that led her to a life of public service and love of nature.

When she was twelve, Beverly was stricken with polio and was told by doctors that she would never walk again. Something clicked in the little girl from Liberal, because she was inspired by an unseen force to fight through arduous months of rehabilitation, learning to "appreciate and value every person, to recognize the interconnectedness of all and to understand that each one of us has something very special to contribute," as she would tell me, including the animals in her life. A dog named Skipper and a cat named Tiger saw her through the dark days, giving her a sense that all living things have value and are connected.

Her first job in the late 1950s was in Santa Monica, working for the famed Douglas Aircraft Company. Several mergers and acquisitions later, the company emerged, just a year before I met her, as Boeing. Beverly found herself in command of the Employees Community Fund, a philanthropy that made over $100 million in grants and scholarships during her tenure in the areas of human services, health, education, environment, services for children and seniors, and the arts. She was always quick to utilize her network to rally around a cause.

"I'll do whatever I can," Beverly volunteered, as we glided toward the dock. "I can call around to the various universities and whale watching groups, even one I visited in Hawaii once, to see what they suggest we do with our orphan. We humans have killed so many of these whales, now it's our turn to save this one."

"I'm going to call the other Keepers to see if they've ever had a whale rescue before," Kris said, as she deftly jumped off the boat and tied us to the rusty cleats on the old wooden dock. There were Keepers in four other southern California counties, so one of them may have ideas or resources we could use.

As the two women clambered off the boat and headed to the BayKeeper headquarters in the adjacent houseboat, "Earthman" David Garcia, a Fox TV news reporter, scurried down the gangway and shouted to catch our attention. He had heard of the morning's events and asked if he could get a ride out to where he and his cameraman might film the action. We shoved off and turned the boat back

Figure 4: *Earthman David Garcia*

towards the open ocean as David peppered me with questions to get a sense of what had taken place so far.

David was a remarkable man on so many levels. A ruddy brown face topped with an elegant shock of white hair, always dressed in safari-style cargo jacket and pants, he had created a persona around reporting environmental stories before they were commonplace or cool. The consummate pro on camera, he spoke to you—not to a TV audience, but to you, one to one. He learned his craft covering Jimmy Carter's White House and later all things South America, but his passion, his purpose, was most certainly focused on tracking the clues of a vanishing natural resource base, fundamental building blocks of our lives on a planet that was rapidly changing.

"We won't get great shots in this fog," David sighed, noting that although it was approaching noon, the sun was barely visible as a gauzy light hovering above a clinging fog that would not likely burn off today. "You won't find the pod in this mess either, I'm guessing."

David had quickly come to the same conclusion as I had that morning, having no other suggestions about how one might rescue a whale without a mother to feed it. He had done many stories on the gray whale migrations and had visited their calving lagoons in Mexico, so I pumped him for any scrap of information that might uncover some trick survival switch we might flip to the "ON" position.

"Well grays are not the largest of whales," he began with his slightly accented Texas drawl. "But they'd certainly earn a spot at the adult table if its kin gathered for Thanksgiving. If she lives to old age, she could grow to fifty feet and tip the scales at forty tons, or about the equivalent of eight African elephants. You'd think a creature that had evolved over millions of years to be so large and with few natural predators would pass the shores on annual migrations immune from the slings and arrows of outrageous fortune that makes most other life forms humble and forgotten. But humans are efficient and abundant predators, so JJ's thousands of years of ancestry were nearly wiped out in little more than a generation of our own."

David's poetic style of speaking and his deep baritone made even useless information seem important. I absorbed what he was saying, realizing that none of it offered a clue of how to help this animal, but did add a sense of obligation to get involved. In Two Years Before the Mast, Richard Henry Dana noted that in 1836 "all the open ports along the coast [were] filled with whales that had come in to make their annual visit...so common that we took little notice of them." After whalers discovered the calving grounds in Baja, it took only about forty years to push them to the brink of extinction. No one can change that history, but as Beverly said, we could save at least this one.

As we approached her again, I was able to pay closer attention to JJ's overall features. She was as sleek as a torpedo, but shaped like a

bloated boomerang, her mottled dark-to-light gray rubbery skin interrupted only by the characteristic irregular knobby ridge on her back.
Her head appeared V-shaped from above, concealing a graceful upper jaw that curved downward ending in a distinct overbite. From our
perspective on the boat, her most apparent feature was the blowhole,

Figure 5: *Adult gray whale shuterstock*

spewing salt spray a dozen feet into the air. In time, a ton of white
barnacles and sea lice would reside in clusters on her head and chin like
an old man's scruffy hair and whiskers. Her mouth would fill with bris-
tling baleen to strain ocean mud for food. For now, she was smooth
as a human baby's bottom, equally toothless and dependent on others.

Despite his years and many adventures, like the rest of us, David
became a child on Christmas morning when JJ rubbed against the boat
and rolled over to meet his gaze. What is it about first contact, about
seeing the living embodiment of a thousand photos and an endless
parade of drawings, charts, and whale statistics?

"Oh, c'mon," he uttered quietly, almost to himself. "We've gotta
keep you alive, little girl."

"So David, in truth, do we simply know too little about gray whales in general to figure out how to help a baby this young?" I asked. "I mean, is there any chance she would skip the nursing phase and figure out how to eat adult food?"

"No," David replied patiently, his gaze and hands never leaving JJ. "Mostly because she's a baby and doesn't know any other way to feed than looking for a teat, but also because there's not much here for her to eat. Gray whales feed off the Arctic Ocean floor, sifting acres and acres of mud every summer, straining out and eating the amphipods. Grays build up so much blubber that they survive the next six months without eating much more. It's ironic that this survival technique may have been their undoing—it's why whalers sought them out for the massive amounts of oil they contained."

Unlike dolphins or killer whales, JJ's kin don't seem to be members of an intricate society or clan, but would her survival also depend on the simple bond of mother and calf? On communicating with others in a migrating pod? On seeing others like her in their natural habitat and imitating their actions and reactions?

"BayKeeper Patrol, this is BayKeeper Base, come in please," the radio squawked suddenly, interrupting the gray whale natural history lesson that David was conducting for me.

"BayKeeper Patrol, go ahead Base," I replied, watching David's cameraman bounce a large video camera atop his shoulder while trying valiantly to avoid fouling the waters around JJ with the contents of his stomach.

"Terry, we've got a problem," Kris said hesitantly over the radio. "I got a call here from Joe Cordaro at National Marine Fisheries. He said to stay away from the whale."

I paused to hear the rest of the message, but the radio went silent. "Huh? That was it?" I asked.

"Well, he also said we would be violating federal law to get within a hundred yards of her and could be fined or arrested if we did. Um... but that was about it."

There was obviously more than food, water, or a good role model to worry about if JJ was going to live.

Chapter 2

THE SEA OF DREAMS

A bit more than a year earlier, JJ's mother cruised the protected warm waters of San Ignacio Lagoon in Baja, about six hundred miles south of San Diego on the Pacific coast. As a whaler in the 1800s saw it, her kind would be one of many that "gather in large numbers, passing and repassing into and out of the estuaries, or slowly raising their colossal forms midway above the surface, falling over on their sides as if by accident, and dashing the water into foam and spray about them." It would appear to be play, like any other vacationer wintering in Mexico.

Not unlike human beach-goers, she too spent pleasant hours doing absolutely nothing, floating calmly at the surface, quite motionless, keeping one position for an hour or more, basking under a warm subtropical sun, the waterline punctuated by the occasional head of a sea turtle or a leathery fisherman in a dilapidated skiff working his nets, lines, or traps. A gull alighted on her motionless body to survey the waterscape for signs of food, preening and peering off into a cloudless blue sky that merged in the distance with vast expanse of tidal flats and mangrove swamps, melting into the pure white sand and salt desert plain weighted by shimmering heat, a landscape interrupted only by vicious washboard dirt roads and scrawny coyotes.

Marina, as we might call her in anticipation of her bearing JJ the following year in Marina del Rey, had an urgent biological agenda that belied the apparent casualness of this idyllic tableau. She was listening carefully to the other whales in the broad lagoon as they squeezed air through their blow holes in short bursts from deep in their lungs. Some whales can be heard over a thousand miles of ocean with voices like violins or sopranos reaching operatic summits many times higher than a human, but Marina's kin squeaked and snorted with grunts and songs in ranges very familiar to the human ear.

Thump…thump…thump…thump like the flat of a hand on a big drum, muffled by distance…

whistle…

grunt…

blip-blip-blip like soap bubbles bursting in the air…

baritone rumble.

Repeat.

The grays in the lagoon talked continuously, day and night, their chatter growing louder when they encountered danger or obstacles, sometimes simply rapid clicks like a thumbnail running along the teeth of a comb. But Marina was in no danger, nor were her companions. Instead they were using their "indoor voices," their muted lagoon whispers and gossips, eager females seeking proud males. Sex was on their minds.

JJ's father may have given her the stubborn determination to succeed, to survive, that would mark her first hours of life. She may not have inherited such genes from Marina, an inexperienced mother who gave birth too early and left her offspring to make its own way in unfamiliar waters. But her father was bold and aggressive, a male who could fend off other suitors and mate with the coy young Marina.

The stillness of the lagoon was shattered all of a sudden, a great tail slapping the surface as the first male closed in on Marina. She coyly rolled over to keep her genitals out of reach, even as a second and a third male vied for her attention.

Bump…

rub…

slap…

roll.

Soon five males surrounded her, each with impressive erections, some pointing straight up into the air as if to impress and intimidate. New England in the day of Melville called the whale's penis "grandissimus" and Ahab's men would remove the skin and use it as a raincoat, cutting two holes for their arms in the sheath, protecting them from blubber and blood as they butchered the rest of the whale.

JJ's father butted a competitor off to one side and ran a fluke across Marina's belly. A younger male had been recruited to support the dominant one, pushing him from below to help him make the crucial connection. Marina rolled over towards her suitor, rubbing her genital opening against his massive beige penis, distinctive among whales, that organ on all other species being dark colored. Groping, pushing, throbbing, not unlike teenagers in the back of dad's Buick.

As they mated, the other males pressed against their bodies to keep them together and await their own turn amidst the churning and thrashing, nothing languorous or Victorian about this mighty act of procreation. Marina might have mated already with several males and she might yet mate with others. But JJ's father had succeeded. His daughter would carry on his genes, her birth a year in the future on a cold day in the waters of the Santa Monica Bay, a world away from the heat and timeless passion of her conception.

Her primary task completed, Marina would soon follow her instincts to begin the migration north, more than six thousand miles, to feeding grounds in the Arctic where she could nourish her own body and the new life growing inside her. She would retrace those miles and return south in time to give birth, although JJ would arrive too soon for a normal gray whale childhood in Mexico. What would that journey be like? What would Marina see, feel, taste, smell in an ocean that bears less and less resemblance to the ocean of her parents and their parents?

We are all drawn to Marina's world, the sea, yet we know less about it than the surface of the moon. Oceans are like outer space to us—dark, cold, filled with alien life and never the same twice, always in motion when you glance from moment to moment, when you sail upon them inch by inch. Beneath the waves, life and water move, change, rise, and sink like snowflakes, no moment ever the same as another.

Sure, Jacques Cousteau's TV magic showed us the undersea world first hand, but even he asked more questions than he answered. New life forms are discovered in the oceans every year, proving again how much there is yet to learn, and only in this generation have we learned than Man can destroy this vast wilderness. For example, almost all commercial fisheries are now in collapse from taking more than Nature can provide, damaging the ability of the ecosystem to recover, while human-made greenhouse gases alter the very chemistry of seawater.

Consider just those two examples of how one species—humans—have profoundly changed the largest habitat on Earth in not much more than a century. We have wiped out sixty, seventy, eighty percent of many of the ocean's animal populations and changed the fundamental makeup of their surroundings in the process. And these two examples only begin to catalogue the ways we are heaping injury upon insult to this ecosystem that is so vital to our own survival.

Perhaps it is that mostly invisible changeability that alienates us from the ocean. Like most people, I can describe the land, in part because it changes slowly or not at all. From visits or photos, I have a sense of the Grand Canyon and Mt. Everest, the Australian outback and the waterfalls of Hawaii. I can also describe what humans have done on the land, such as the Tower of London and the smog of Los Angeles, the Great Wall of China and rows upon rows of corn in Kansas. I could populate long lists with the places I've been and the things I've seen on that thirty percent of the globe, but am hard-pressed to describe, in anything like that amount of detail, the thing that covers the other seventy percent—the ocean.

In fact there are no "oceans," no colored lines in the vast saltwater mountains and canyons, deserts and farms, that divide the Sargasso from the Atlantic or the Pacific from the Indian. Oceans are a man-made conceit. There is but one great blanket that covers more than two-thirds of our earthly bed. What if we could ride on Marina's back along her epic twelve thousand mile tour of the eastern Pacific? What would be revealed to us then?

Had Marina taken us on such a tour when Earth was young, there would have been no boundaries of any kind. Oceans covered all of the earth four billion years ago, soon after planet creation. Microscopic life formed in those oceans 3.8 billion years ago and, as land emerged about two hundred fifty million years ago, it was as one large landmass, a single island in a great sea. About the time dinosaurs appeared a hundred million years later, give or take, that single land mass broke apart and began to drift into today's continents, creating tidepools and coastal wetlands, fecund laboratories for the evolution of complex plant and animal species.

Despite this common heritage of all earthly life forms, science has largely excluded the oceans from most of humanity's academic inquiries. Fish pre-date both dinosaurs and humans by hundreds of millions of years, yet it has only been in the last hundred years that we learned very much about them and the place they inhabit. For example, it wasn't until the first decade of the 20TH century when we learned that photosynthesis doesn't take place deeper than a hundred feet below the surface. Nor was it a celebrated marine biologist or trail-blazing oceanographer who made this profound discovery, but a Frenchman who photographed "hysterical" women for a living and just dabbled in studies of the sea. Virtually nothing was known of anything deeper than that until the 1970s. Marina's world has long been a mystery to humans and certainly this ignorance has contributed to our treatment of the ocean and the decline of its health.

And if we don't know the ocean, we can't know ourselves. We are of the ocean in every meaningful sense. The first living organisms to convert sunlight into food are the same blue-green algae in the ocean today—1.7 billion years old and the base of our own food chain. The first sex and reproduction on earth took place in the ocean, among sponges and jellyfish, igniting the Darwinian processes that evolved into land animals and homo sapiens. An 1855 account of the sea called it "a dynamic whole...as perfect and harmonious as the atmosphere or the blood," which turned out to be quite literally true—humans and the surface of the earth are both made up of about two thirds saltwater.

To know the ocean in a physical sense, especially Marina's slice of the Pacific, open an atlas to the pages that show North America on the right and the Pacific Ocean on the left. If you could erase the blue from the ocean page you would see a mirror image of the mountains, deserts, and Great Plains that you see on the land page. Look carefully and you will also see great "cities" on the left page, mirroring Los Angeles, New Orleans, and New York on the right page—ocean communities of billions of creatures, some in dense high-rise sea mounts, others spread across great plains in sparse solitude. Land-based creatures on the right compare with bottom-dwellers on the left; vast flocks of migratory birds and insects populating the air on the right com-

pare with bountiful schools of plankton and fish swimming through the water column on the left. When your mind's eye has captured the images of the communities and structures of both, cover the left page with blue water once more. Now you know what lies beneath.

Marina began her migration on that blue page from the tidepools within the lagoons of Baja Mexico. No other place on earth experiences such drastic changes

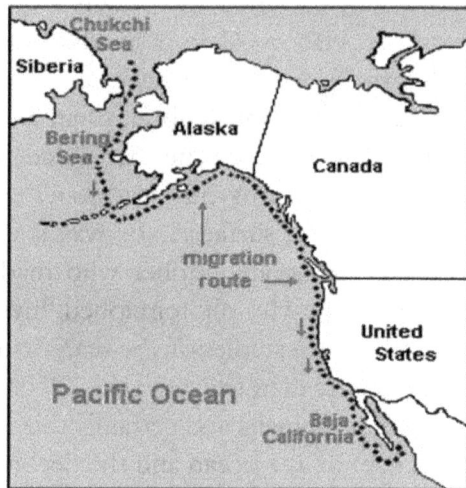

Figure 6: *Gray whale migration*

in habitat as these warm waters where dry changes to wet, freezing turns to hot, shaded to exposed, calm to pounding waves. To survive, all life forms there must be designed to withstand those forces and prevent desiccation when the life-giving water recedes twice each day. Mussels know to open and feed when submerged, but close securely after capturing cool waters within their shells for survival during low tide. Colorful anemones cover themselves with white stones to reflect the heat of the sun as the water recedes. Tidewater goby are graced with larger gills to maximize their oxygen collection in the shallow, fickle waters. Even simple algae in the tidal zone become more gelatinous than their deep-water relatives to retain moisture when exposed to the air for so many hours each day.

Out of the sheltered lagoons and swimming north, parallel to this intricate ecosystem, Marina gracefully curled and thrust her great tail in symphony with surf, tides, wind, and sun, mile by mile towards her banquet in the Arctic. Crossing the invisible ocean border between Mexico and the US, she passed another kind of fenceline to her right—a dense green/brown row of sentinels reaching fifty, sixty, seventy feet from the rocky bottom to the surface. Gracefully undulating kelp forests, a protective tangle of cabbage heads, leather neckties, and feather boas, sheltering the fantastic and familiar alike—sea otters that play, eat, and wrap their babies in a swaddling of kelp to keep them from drifting towards the shore and the merciless waves pounding on the rocks; spiny purple urchins, eerie rays, sharp-toothed eels, and halibut peering up from the sediment below; crabs that collect ocean litter for disguises; slugs that eat poisonous anemones and secrete the toxins through their own skin to ward off predators; schools of transparent possum shrimp hiding their young in pouches like their namesakes; male hermit crabs carrying around females on their shells in the protected confines of the root-like holdfast, tapping shell to shell until she emerges for mating.

Marina swam in and out of these great forests, opportunistically feeding on shrimp and enjoying the sensations of a thousand rubbery hands massaging her bulk. Off to her left lay deeper waters, a string of Grand Canyons dropping off more than three thousand feet and bearing names on maps irrelevant to any gray whale, like Scripps, Santa Monica, Monterey, and Willapa, all along her steady journey northward. Dangers lurked in those deeper waters, so instinct kept her slaloming from kelp beds to open ocean but always at a distance from the deep, like a cautious tourist on the edge of a great precipice. As winds blew the surface water offshore, the colder water rose from below, cooling Marina's belly, even as the lengthening hours of sunlight warmed her long, dark back.

Figure 7: *Gray whale breaching*

She made her way not just between shallow and deep or cool and warm, but also between the visible and the invisible. If the earth were a basketball, the atmosphere would be like a sheet of the thinnest paper. The thickness of the ocean would be thinner yet. And thinner still—like the moisture from your breath on the basketball and no more—the microlayer—the skin of the ocean, an ecosystem in plain sight yet hidden from most human insight.

Marina rose and fell across this unseen boundary, a hair-thin place where air meets water and creates a distinctive home to plankton, crab larvae, a thousand forms of algae, and the miraculous mechanical and chemical processes that transfer oxygen to and from the depths. Without the microlayer, nothing would survive in the ocean, the most delicate link in a chain of unimaginable intricacy. We also depend on the bounty of the microlayer—if gases can't penetrate the surface of the water, because, for example, it is coated with an oil spill, then oxygen can't escape back out of the ocean and into the atmosphere. Animals that rely on breathing oxygen, including whales and humans, would all soon suffocate, because so much of that life-sustaining gas is produced in the sea.

Marina gave no hint that the wildly varying environments were either familiar or alien to her, but rather pushed through all of them without leaving a trace of her passage, keeping the shore in sight when she breached, traveling mostly in a straight line, weeks becoming months, covering twenty miles a day from Baja to Big Sur, not slowing by day or night. As Marina swam, her senses were always alert for the only real peril that lay along the route, indeed the only real reason to favor the coast and not the open ocean, making her long migration even longer. Marina's clicks and songs, at times returned by other migrating grays, would go silent for only one reason—the presence of killer whales.

Killer whales—orcas—sleek black and white bodies patrol in wolf-packs along the entire eastern Pacific, especially northern California to Alaska. Looking for the young or the weak, they know their best chance for a kill will be in open waters, over the canyons along Marina's route, lying in wait to come unseen from the deep where there is no place to hide. At the southern edge of Monterey Bay, the last great natural feature before San Francisco Bay, Marina sensed or heard the presence of orcas. She slowed her breathing and movements, silenced all communications, drifted slowly to the surface only to briefly expose her blowhole to gently exhale and quietly inhale, one submariner trying to escape detection by another.

Orcas are not true whales, but rather the largest of the dolphins, growing up to thirty feet and ten tons. Size is not the only difference between orcas and other dolphins—gray whales bear no scars from Flipper, but about half of the gray whale population does bear the scars of orca attacks, especially on flukes and flippers, throats and snouts. These scars bear witness to the aggressiveness of orcas, but also to their shrewd, efficient tactics. Injure the limbs and killing the prey becomes easier. Grab it by the snout and pull it under, it drowns.

Mother grays and their calves typically migrate north in kelp beds and shallows to Point Lobos at Monterey Bay, where the drop off exceeds ten thousand feet. If they take the short cut across the bay, orcas wait. If they hug the shoreline, the long months of hunger grow even longer. Not all orcas will attack grays—one type eats fish and communicates constantly with frequency-modulated whistles in a very social community. The second type, called "transients," are stealthy hunters that feed primarily on marine mammals of all types. Both groups patrol the eastern Pacific coast, but genetics show they haven't inter-bred for at least a thousand centuries. Like Athenians and Spartans, one tribe bred for society and the other for war.

Cruising without a calf, Marina's natural instinct to get to her food source quickly overrode any doubts about crossing the Monterey Bay Canyon. A pod of grays just ahead of her must also have felt safe, swimming unusually close together twenty-seven strong. They passed small groups of "Athenian" orcas, but their luck was an illusion as sixteen "Spartan" orcas organized an attack nearby with military precision.

First, the aggressive pod of orcas created a crescent formation and synchronized their breathing so they would all be at the surface or in the depths at the same time, always retaining the benefit of the group. Instinct divided them into platoons as they moved towards the weakest of the grays, the easiest kills, attacking from all sides trying to separate mothers and calves.

The grays organized too, breaking up into compact defensive groups of three, ready to roll together like floating logs to stymie any attempt by an orca to grab onto a gray's fluke or tail. Neither made a sound for a time as grays eluded orcas, but the predator patiently closed distance on prey.

When the orcas struck, the attack came from below, marked by a mother orca that relentlessly nipped at a gray whale calf over and over again. The mother gray rolled rapidly, bumping into the aggressor, trying to prevent it from getting a firm grip on her offspring, finally rolling onto her back and taking the calf on her belly to hold it above the reach of the attackers. When she could hold her breath no more, when she herself was being bitten from all sides, she rolled over and released her baby to its fate.

The mother orca leapt over the gray whale calf to push it below the surface, teaching her own offspring to ride the helpless infant like a horse in order to drown it. Another orca wedged its snout into the mouth of the gray to seize the tongue, the massive bloodletting that followed a technique designed to weaken and kill the prey quickly.

A whaler in the 1800s observed that the attack of the orca on a gray "may be likened…to a pack of hounds holding the stricken deer at bay. They cluster about the animal's head, some of their number breaching over it, while others seize it by the lips and haul the bleeding monster under water; and when captured, should the mouth be open, they eat out its tongue." Once separated from the tired, bleeding, and disoriented mother, the baby gray's life was over.

After the kill, the orcas worked with practiced teamwork on the feeding, one stripping blubber while others held the carcass in place, much as their ancestors had done for generations as also reported by the old whaler. "As soon as the prize had settled to the bottom, the orcas descended, bringing up large pieces of flesh in their mouths, which they devoured after coming to the surface." Even a baby gray is a massive feast, so much meat that the orcas leave the bulk of it for the sharks, scavengers, and opportunistic schools of fish.

Marina must have been aware of the carnage off to her left in deeper waters. A sentient being, but also a sensitive one? Was she unnerved by what she heard, smelled, and may have seen? Did it have added meaning if any of the grays in the pod ahead were acquaintances from Baja? Was the father of the calf growing inside her among them?

Off to the west, just beyond the orcas' kill zone, lay the great Pacific, millions of square miles, an underwater continent of natural wonders that mirror the topographical map of North American. Although the deep rifts could easily be mistaken for the Grand Canyon and the towering mountains would rival the sharp-edged Sierras, in between lay acre after featureless acre of oozing flat bottom.

No greater or less inspiring than the endless plains of Kansas and the Dakotas on land, it is this simple sediment in the ocean, never seen by most of Earth's human population, that is our planet's most predominant feature—almost a third of the world is covered by mud. Vast plains, but far from empty—inhabited by urchins, micro-organisms, crabs, flatfish, eels, giant foot-long lice-like isopods, all engaged in feeding frenzies when the remains of a baby gray whale fall to the bottom, like piranhas, leaving only bleached bones as testament to its abbreviated existence.

These great mud flats are punctuated by volcanoes sporting four hundred degree plumes of black sulfides, toxic to most life forms, but which surprisingly nourish an array of bacteria, shrimp, worms, eels, and squat lobsters, all colorless beings in a world devoid of natural light, a world that gains no energy from the sun, only from these mysterious vents in the dark, some taller than Everest, some that create towering ghost towns when their volcanoes fall silent.

Nautilus and squid rise up along these peaks by night, like vampires, to the reefs that clad the base of volcanic islands, feeding and quickly returning to the darkness of depth by day. They are joined by great clouds of plankton that rise and fall to the same beat of tide and time, seeking food of their own, then floating peacefully like snow from the sky, mixed in with detritus from above, an oceanic blizzard that feeds shrimp, tiny fish, and plants at the base of a food chain, which in turn nourish sea creatures and humans alike, a slow-motion banquet, more than a month in transit to the sea floor thousands of feet below.

In shallow waters, the ocean is a riot of color, but at such intimidating depths, the ocean is robbed of this palette as light is absorbed until there is nothing but absolute black. Making these scenes even more extra-terrestrial, the cold light of bioluminescence is occasionally visible, like the first streaks of sunrise on a foggy day, produced by bacteria, plankton, and vampire squid, sometimes only emitted in the wake of a passing whale or giant squid, appearing as sparkles, pulses, eruptions, and ghostly seas. Faintly illuminated moon jellies hover in the water column, growing or shrinking many times their size as food comes or goes, snatching tiny shrimp on minuscule hairs and slowly conveying them to their mouths, like a mosh pit passing a concert goer across the audience.

As April showers swelled coastal rivers north of San Francisco, Marina cruised past the land-based symbols of another fundamental power of the ocean—it's life-sustaining food supply. Giant redwoods, thousands of years old and hundreds of feet high, hovering above half-ton elk and great bears feeding on fatty salmon the size of sled dogs, all grown to such proportions from the largesse of the sea.

Salmon spawn in fresh water streams that don't have the resources to grow the juveniles to anything approaching their massive adult size, so the young fish swim to the ocean, miraculously transforming their body chemistry from fresh water creatures to salt water. There, in the ocean wilderness, they spend years hunting in the seemingly endless bounty of the sea. As huge adults, they return to the streams of their nativity to repay their own genetic debt and, in the process, deliver the ocean's vast quantities of nutrients to the forests.

After spawning, the salmon die, their fat and flesh providing food for bears, birds, insects, and a dozen other forest denizens. Scavengers pull carcasses deeper into the forest. These animals, in turn, fertilize the land and complete the most astonishing transfer of wealth on the planet—nutrients from the sea that allow trees to grow to such massive proportions, trees that then protect the streams for another generation of salmon to begin the process anew. Many humans have also grown fat on this bounty, feeding from the plants and animals of the forest, although early white explorers didn't share the native taste for the salmon itself. Lewis and Clark caught salmon and traded it to locals for dog meat, a food that apparently more appealed to their European palates, much to the amazement of local Indians along the Columbia River in Oregon.

As Marina passed the halfway point in her six thousand mile journey, hunger became an equal motivation to fear. She picked up her pace, risking deep water passages, sensing that her feeding grounds were getting closer. The pod ahead crossed her path and stopped at Oregon's Depoe Bay to feed on shrimp in the kelp beds and perhaps to regain their sense of security after the orca attack. Marina stayed offshore, rhythmically thrusting, ambivalent to cold, current, orcas, or other distractions.

Marina instinctively sought help from the ocean's vast highway of currents, slow lanes and fast, used by both whales and humans for transport, temperature regulation, weather, and food. These currents form giant conveyor belts, continents of cold clear water within warm, silty waters at varying depths, encircling the globe, moving warmth and food on a three-dimensional chess board, numerous migrant species moving up or down the water column to find propulsion in the right direction, like a shopper seeking the right escalator in a vast mall.

Nor did she stop as others do after crossing the Straight of Juan de Fuca, to feed on ghost shrimp off Whidbey Island. Instead, after passing from US waters to Canadian, she maintained her course and speed with other goals in mind. If she had stopped in any of the estuaries along the coast of British Columbia, she might have seen the occasional carcass of an old or sick gray that had meandered up river in search of solace or sustenance, dying unnoticed, their flesh quickly converted to nutrients for bears, eagles, fish, and towering forests. Slowing neither by day or night, Marina now covered eighty miles a day, four times the pace that she swam upon leaving the warm lagoons many weeks ago

The last days of spring behind her, Marina used the Inside Passage between Vancouver Island and the British Columbia mainland as a safe highway to the north, sharing it with ferry boats and fishers, both man and animal seeking protection as they traveled. Breaking out to open waters at the southern end of Alaska, perhaps following the scent trail of the others that swam ahead, Marina gave Prince William Sound a wide berth, a phenomena among grays observed only since the infamous Exxon Valdez oil spill six years before.

Some grays begin to slow their pace, feeding on whatever can be found in the muds off the Alaskan coast, but others avoid the Pacific side of the Aleutian Islands—military dumping has left a toxic moonscape that has affected seals and whales as they pass. As Marina looked for passage between the islands, a rocket launched from nearby Kodiak Island, pounding and rumbling the air and water, fouling the tideline with hydrochloric acid and toxic clouds of dust.

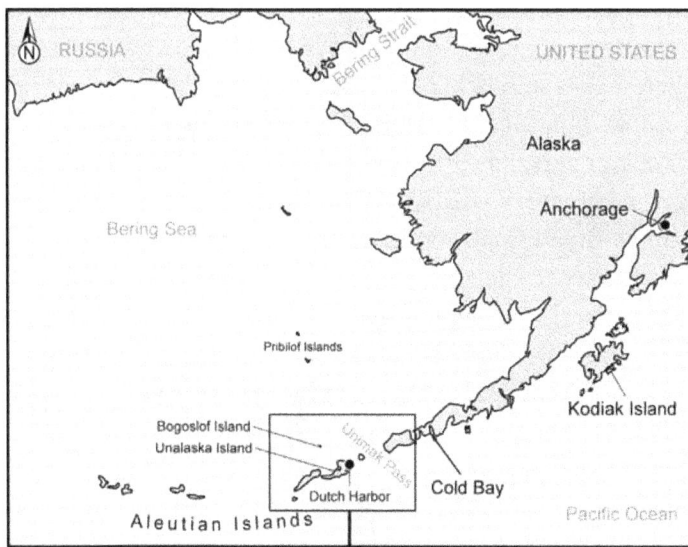

Figure 8: *Kodiak Island and Unimak Pass*

At Unimak Island, Marina found a long, crowded line of immigrants bustling to get through the picket fence of islands, one of the few favored passages to the north. Cruising within a stone's throw of shore, she circumnavigated the throng and was at last in the cold waters of the Bering Sea.

The water temperature on Marina's journey had gone from the mid-sixties in Baja to sub-freezing in the Arctic, but the cold was a welcome signal to start feeding. Diving to the bottom over and over again, straining great gulps of mud for the feast of ocean insects it contained. When she had arrived in Mexico last winter, there was less than eight hours of light in a day; now in the Arctic summer, it was nearly never dark. For the last months of summer, Marina would feed and grow fat, as did the baby JJ inside her.

Like other pregnant females, she headed south a month or so before most of the grays, leaving these grounds in October to retrace her route, avoiding the hazards, riding the currents, gaining any advantage she could to get to warm water before giving birth. Another six thousand miles and more, another five months or longer, before returning to the safety of the Baja lagoon.

But Marina couldn't wait. A few weeks shy of achieving her goal, somewhere near the bustle of modern Los Angeles, she answered the ancient call and gave birth to her calf, leaving the newborn to the care of human strangers, left on a sandy doorstep in Marina del Rey.

"Yes, a baby gray whale," Kris assured a reporter who had called several times already, pausing to listen to his next question. "No, Free Willy was a killer whale, an orca," she said patiently, glad that Beverly hadn't left yet and was helping her with the phones. She regretted that the official site visit about our grant was cut short, but suspected the experience they shared that morning had made a very strong impression on Beverly anyway.

Why are so many people, like Kris and Beverly, drawn to the sea? People who surf, people who fish, even people who can't swim. Beaches draw more people than amusement parks. Explorers seek sunken treasure and new forms of life. Children build whimsical castles in wet sand long before imagining their dream homes in the suburbs. Are we called home? Do we make connections when we arrive?

"When we got to her, she seemed small, delicate, and vulnerable," Kris told the reporter. "It really felt like a baby that was lost. She seemed gentle, friendly."

Lost. Gentle. Friendly. Who among us will not respond to a baby that meets that description? Kris was born at a hospital in Walnut Creek, California, named for the famous naturalist John Muir, so perhaps her community imprinted her at birth to care for the wild. Walnut Creek was a small, sleepy, average working class town east of San Francisco. Like many such towns, it couldn't contain its citizens' aspirations in the 1960s as seismic shifts changed the fundamental relationship of people to the roots of their being. Kris and her family moved to Australia, where the little girl, fearful and inspired, adopted an Aussie accent to blend in, to become a part of the new fabric of an adopted sense of community.

Within a few years, even the great "down under" couldn't contain her family and they moved again, peeling back even more layers from the post-war sense of conformity, this time to Rio de Janiero. Like many idealized hopes of anti-establishment living, Rio turned out to be violent, corrupt, and expensive. A year in Toronto seemed more manageable, white Christmas, ice-skating, and first experience with cold weather, but within months, the Haddads gravitated back to Walnut Creek. Perhaps that bold round trip migration at an early age gave Kris some instinctive connection to baby JJ, also carried by a parent with wanderlust for thousands of miles into unknown waters.

Or did her bond with nature and other life forms germinate from her frequent travels to the nearby Smith River—home to the giant redwoods, rocky coastlines, and pristine rivers? Whatever its roots, Kris remained calibrated more to the rhythms of the wild than the metropolis, despite college and an early career in advertising in San Francisco. A passion for acting lured her to Los Angeles, but her visceral need to be woven into a greater fabric led her to answer the call for a job with an environmental activist organization—the Santa Monica BayKeeper—taking on research, coordinating volunteers, fundraising, boat patrols, and, on truly unique days, rescuing errant baby gray whales.

"OK, I think I have a good list of the marine biology programs in California and I'll start by calling them to see what they think we should do," Beverly told Kris as she packed up her notes and stuffed them into her oversized purse. "I have to get to the office, but let's talk at the end of the day and see where we stand."

"You know, when I thought of whales before, in the abstract, well until I met JJ, they seemed blue, grey, peaceful, giant, wise, kinglike, evolved, enlightened, magnificent, source of life and inspiration," Kris said, helping Beverly off the houseboat deck and down onto the dock. "But then there were also images in my head from Moby Dick—sad, old, large, rough seas; and from Free Willy—kind, peace-loving, gentle. JJ defies all of these stereotypes, maybe because she's just a huge baby in need of a lot of help to survive."

"Hang in there," Beverly advised, noting that a few tears were welling up in Kris' eyes at the thought that they might not be able to help this unusual orphan. "We'll come up with something."

Kris felt some hope, simply because a woman of Beverly's strength and experience was willing to help the upstart BayKeeper outfit. Although it was now nearly noon, the air remained chilly and damp, so she quickly turned back inside, to her desk and the incessant ringing of the phones. She noticed the flashing red light that signaled another message had been left while she was saying goodbye to Beverly. She had a feeling there would be a lot of messages on the BayKeeper Hotline as more reporters covered the unfolding drama of cetacean life and death. The familiar clicks and beeps of the message machine gave way to the stern, clipped voice of a man.

Joe Cordaro identified himself as a representative of the National Marine Fisheries Service. His message was blunt and unequivocal. Federal law prohibits you from approaching the whale and under no circumstances are you to attempt any "rescue." If you do, you will all be prosecuted. He didn't leave a number.

Somewhat unnerved, like seeing the red lights in your rear view mirror for no apparent reason, Kris radioed me on the patrol boat with the news. As her voice bounced from the loudspeaker across the water, a loud, cynical laugh bounced back from behind me.

"Aw fuck him," Peter Wallerstein chuckled. He had slowly drawn his Whale Rescue Team boat closer to my location, quiet and careful to avoid disturbing the whale, but now close enough to hear the radio transmission. "Joe's not the one looking this little orphan in the eye right now, is he?"

I was relieved to see Peter on the scene, both because he had a lot of experience rescuing whales and dolphins, but also because he had experience dealing with marine mammal law and the bureaucracy behind it. JJ rolled over and slowly glided over to Peter's gray inflatable Zodiac, probing the underside for a nipple as she had done with my boat. Peter made eye contact and stroked her side, his body leaning mostly outside the confines of the boat, defying gravity and hovering over the infant whale like a spirit. His connection to her was forged from many such encounters and seemed instantly like a familiar relative greeting the newest addition to the family.

"She looks better than when we found her in the surf this morning," Peter observed clinically. "But without milk she won't make it to tomorrow…gotta find mom."

As muted midday sunlight fought in vain to push back the mist, it became apparent that JJ's survival also depended on keeping the growing flotilla of spectator boats from running over her. Peter and I now used Cordaro's warning to the onlookers—come any closer and you will be arrested—to create an invisible force field around our boats and JJ. She swam from one boat to the other, alternately looking for a nipple and engaging in what simply seemed like play. Was she both hungry and bored, like any infant in a playpen, looking for food and kinship, something to feed both her body and mind? She flapped her tail awkwardly now and again, like a child holding its hand in front of its face and taking delight in wiggling the fingers and forming the basic elements of a fist. Each time she approached Peter's boat, then mine, she rolled over briefly to make eye contact, then bumped the side and bottom of the vessels, rubbing, scraping, splashing, and exhaling with equal vigor.

"Hey Peter," I called out as our boats drifted farther apart. "Why don't you stay with the whale and I go out to look for the pod? Maybe if we can find the mother—or any other whales—we can lure them back together."

Peter probably knew my idea was silly, his experience telling him that migrating whales were long gone from the area by now and the chance of finding the mother was equally unlikely as the chance of coaxing the baby to some distant location to reunite with them. Any port in a storm though, so he concurred with the plan and added some encouraging words.

After making sure that JJ was nuzzling Peter's boat and well clear of mine, I restarted my outboard and slowly backed away from the area. First stop was back at the dock to drop off David Garcia and his pitiful green-faced cameraman, whose head had remained poised over the side of the boat for the past hour. I changed jackets, getting one that was warmer and waterproof, and headed out to sea. As I throttled the big engine to push the patrol boat toward the open water, another plan began to crystallize in my mind. If we couldn't find the mother, maybe SeaWorld would take the orphan and nurse it back to health. They had done that for sea lions, I recalled, so why not a baby whale?

Back near the shoreline, Peter was listening to JJ's breathing and hatching a similar plan. But he knew that overcoming federal officials and a marine amusement park, that was focused more on profits than philanthropy, would be equally daunting as my plan of finding a mother whale and reuniting her with JJ. Peter knew what had to be done and steeled himself for what only he knew was yet to come.

Chapter 3

CHOOSING SIDES

Peter Wallerstein gives schizophrenia a good name. He was the "team" of the Whale Rescue Team, every rescuer, naturalist, educator, crewmember, and a sharp-eyed captain rolled into one. Broad shoulders, mop of black hair, garage-sale styling, quick to laugh, and always gives you the sense that there's something he, or you, forgot. His stream of consciousness about his humble beginning almost half a century earlier illuminates the origins of the multiple personalities.

"I was born in Norwalk, Connecticut in 1952, lower middle class Jewish family… left home right after high school, just started traveling around the country, sailed through the West Indies and South America, crewing on sailboats, lived on little uninhabited islands all by myself, kind of searching for what this eighteen, nineteen-year-old kid was going to do in his life, confused, wanted to do something fulfilling in my life…tried just being low impact on the planet…so, from the islands I went to a logger's cabin up on top of a mountain in New Hampshire…no electricity for two years through the winters, self sufficient, grew my own food, bartered with neighbors, lived a simple life, wrote poetry, and just kind of thought, well, this is my way… got involved in some of the issues, the anti-nuke issues and that piece at Seabrook Power Plant, things like that…but it just wasn't enough for me…so I had the urge, I just got in a 1970 Toyota Land Cruiser,

Figure 9: *Author (in boat) and Peter Wallerstein (in water)*

three speed and no top on it, and drove out to California…after all the years of traveling and ended up here, basically, again just searching for something that was fulfilling in my life…a lot of what I do, some of it selfless, some selfish, because I could never settle for just a regular nine-to-five job and unfulfilling, unrewarding life…Whale Rescue Team is that thing…I had seen Sea Shepherd for a couple of years in the media and they were going to have a benefit in Redondo Beach in 1983, so I went down there and Paul Watson was there and I gave him all the money I had right then and there and said, "Listen, I'd like to help"…and the next day they called me up and two weeks after that, I was on the Board of Directors of Sea Shepherd Society, helping coordinate campaigns, just kind of finding my way in there and it felt good because it was hands-on, it wasn't just with a group that was writing letters…back then we're getting out there and sinking whaling ships if we had to, or ramming them in a nonviolent way so nobody would be injured…I really believed in that…to make a statement to stand up for things and to bring attention to things…and from that, I was just home one evening watching the news program, and it was showing a California gray whale drowning in the fishing nets off Palos Verdes…and I made a couple of calls and found out that there was no response…no human response to try to help these animals when they were entangled in the net…so, once they get entangled, they're dead…unless they broke loose but, still they trail the net and get weak and drown anyway…and to me that was unacceptable…so I got a little boat and I said, "I'm going to go out there, man"… somebody has got to try to help the animals and also bring attention to what's happening in our local waters…you're off traveling the, you know, the world's oceans, confronting drift-netters and whaling and sealers, and here we are in our own backyard, a serious problem…so it ended up, one of our first rescue calls, it was a mother and baby gray whale, entangled in the net off Palos Verdes…and when we got out there, we are with all our scuba gear on and we didn't have any books to open up here, so how you free it, a whale entangled in a fishing net…so we had over-kill, too much stuff, kitchen knives, we ended up going out to cut the mother out of the net, but the baby was still entangled…so the mother came up underneath and lifted her baby out of the water half a dozen times, and we eventually cut the net from the baby and they both swim away…just that rewarding and that fulfillment we got, and the satisfaction we got from that, we didn't really know what we were doing but it worked, and it showed me, wow…if this could work then we need to continue doing this…so that was really the birth of the Whale Rescue Team."

Figure 10: *Whale engtangled in fishing net*

All of the roles in that drama, the "we" in his story, are Peter's. Another role, one he spoke of in grey tones, decibels lower than the voices of the other characters, was that of law-breaker. The National Marine Fisheries Service—NMFS—tried repeatedly to shut him down, citing federal law that prohibits anyone from approaching and touching whales, dolphins, sea lions, and other marine mammals, even Good Samaritans with kitchen knives freeing the otherwise doomed. Peter agonizes over the conflict and its potential consequences, but follows his conscience and fights to gain formal approval for his work.

Tension of another kind grew for both of us as Friday morning became afternoon and still every attempt to locate Marina or her pod, every last hope of a natural outcome for her stranded baby, disappeared in the persistent gray seas and foggy skies. My futile patrol to find other whales was quickly ended in fog and rising swells, especially after a news helicopter reported that its crew had flown farther offshore, into clear skies, and seen nothing helpful.

Swarms of onlookers, boaters, surfers on paddleboards, helicopters, and kayakers would all have gladly violated federal law to get close to JJ, to experience contact with a life form that was known to them, yet completely alien as if it had landed on our planet from another. Peter's hundreds of successful rescues had earned him formal marine mammal rescue status from Los Angeles County and various coastal cities, but no such approval from the feds. Neither would my status as the BayKeeper protect me from prosecution if NMFS officials chose to intervene.

In a Los Angeles Sheriff patrol boat, Captain Butler continued to run wide circles around us, an invisible fenceline of flashing lights and megaphone that left no doubt that the infant whale and its two surrogate parents were off limits to the curious. JJ remained playful, rolling and experimenting with flukes, tail, blowhole, and our boats, but her attention soon returned to what must have been a growing hunger as she edged up to Peter's boat hoping to find the elusive nipple. Finding none, she tried the BayKeeper boat again, each time apparently comforted by our stroking and cooing, but certainly confused and maybe a bit irritated.

"She's not going to make it this way," Peter called out. I realized that he was used to freeing an animal or taking the small ones to the rescue center in San Pedro for rehab. He wasn't used to the no-win situation that left him a spectator.

"C'mon, there's got to be a tank somewhere big enough to put her so she can at least get fed," I suggested clumsily. "Or could we create an enclosure out here somehow and get gallons of milk and a hose…" I couldn't finish the thought, knowing how impractical it was.

"SeaWorld," Peter said simply. "But they only give a shit about the ones they can exploit and I don't see this little baby jumpin' through any flaming Hula hoops any time soon."

"But why couldn't they take her for rehab and release her back into the wild?"

"They won't want to and Cordaro won't let them anyhow…they scratch each other's back too much and don't want people to see whales and dolphins stressed and dying from human causes when they both make their money lying about how good we all are to these creatures."

Joe Cordaro was the wildlife biologist for NMFS in southern California. To some, he was the Darth Vader to Peter's Rebel Alliance of one. To many others, Cordaro was doing his job based on laws that he was not allowed to interpret. He would say himself that he struggles with rescues every year, wanting Nature to take its own course except when humans have upset the balance in the first place. Asked to allow the rescue of abandoned seal pups near San Diego, for instance, his response was textbook.

"We don't allow rescues to occur in natural areas," Cordaro told reporters at the time, explaining that the protected cove in La Jolla is a natural sea lion nursery area. "What I have to wrestle with is, if these pups were abandoned naturally or because of human interference— were there indications of disturbance from tourists and commercial photographers."

Dealing with an abandoned gray whale calf would get no special treatment from Cordaro. Asked why there had been a tripling in the usual number of calves born early in southern California waters instead of Mexico, he replied factually.

"We don't know why so many whales are giving birth in California instead of waiting to get down to Baja," Cordaro said. "The whales aren't giving birth early—they're simply not going all the way down to Mexico. We need to let natural survival carry itself out. And if we don't allow it to happen, the population is going to get so big that there's going to be a massive die-off."

Peter and I swapped ideas for still more implausible solutions, our boats rolling back and forth atop the swell, fending off the chill of the insistent mists, until we were left with but one possibility, made manifest by the incessant drumbeat of news choppers overhead. We would make a plea to SeaWorld to rescue baby JJ through the media.

Get the story to every reporter we could contact and ask people to call SeaWorld and Joe Cordaro and demand their help.

If past is prologue, this just might work. SeaWorld had tried to capture a baby gray whale in 1971, ostensibly to "study" the animal. SeaWorld's experts knew the chances of survival for an infant gray whale in captivity were small, but the hopes of a box office hit outweighed the downside of failure, especially in those days before the Marine Mammal Protection Act, which today would prevent them from trying.

In coastal waters, not far from SeaWorld's San Diego theme park, their staff soon located a baby gray whale they would quickly name "Gigi." Gigi's mother put her body between the capture boat and her offspring, much as she would do to fend off attacking orcas, then tried to dive with the infant to avoid capture. Gigi was no match for a quick hand with a nylon noose that went over her head, sliding along her body to the tail and taking her in tow.

Once separated, the mother flailed and slammed her great tail to the water to create havoc, but soon succumbed to her own exhaustion as the SeaWorld hunters towed her baby toward a sling and hoist on the main capture ship. Both mother and calf made rapid clicking and deep breathing sounds of panic never before heard by marine mammal biologists. Secured in the flagship, her captors estimated that the chase had so exhausted Gigi that she would not likely survive. They began plotting another hunt and calculated how they could disorient the next mother, if it also tried so valiantly to separate them from their prize.

When they delivered her to SeaWorld, Gigi was eighteen feet long and weighed in at just over two tons. She was confined to a tank less than twice her length and, predictably, she rejected food or human succor of any kind for two weeks. Like any orphan in a strange world, she was disoriented and scared, losing weight day by day. SeaWorld veterinarians soon realized they simply had no idea what to feed her—their first concoction included fish and whipped cream, perhaps at least one reason that she became violent when humans even entered her tiny tank.

Eager to recoup their investment before it was too late, Gigi was moved in this agitated and declining state to another small tank—but this one in public view. She seemed resigned to her apparent fate, refusing food while becoming visibly more listless and depressed. Pie-faced kids pounded the glass of her tank and pressed gooey noses against it to elicit responses. Hoping to distract the viewers from her obvious distress, and having run out of other tactics to improve her demeanor, SeaWorld added a dolphin to Gigi's tank to attempt some interaction with another living creature.

Whether it was this new companion or the continued variations in food recipes, Gigi began to respond. She ate and tried swimming, although one activity slowly made the other impossible—as she consumed more food and grew to twenty feet, the thirty-five foot tank soon became even more cramped.

SeaWorld's only justification for this harsh confinement was research, but after a year of vets and volunteers in lab coats and wet-suits all around her, the scientific community learned almost nothing of value from Gigi, while their experiments can only be described as animal cruelty. She was poked, prodded, and constrained with contraptions that probed every orifice of her body in ways that would evoke medieval dungeons if the subject were human, including one experiment that essentially smothered the young whale, ostensibly testing her ability to breath. She was stimulated to make sounds for comparison to those recorded in the wild, but in the end she didn't make any recognizable vocalizations until SeaWorld released her from captivity.

Gigi's fate after her release is unknown, but SeaWorld was on the map with the public and the amusement park's coffers were filled, much like Queen Elizabeth sending English pirates to replenish the royal treasury with plunder from the high seas at the expense of other nations. SeaWorld, and a public it wanted to encourage to return again and again, were now addicted to bigger more spectacular animal attractions, which led to the capture and training of more dolphins, sea lions, sea otters, and ultimately their icon, the killer whale "Shamu," played by many hapless orcas over the decades.

"It's not just a park, its another world" is the slogan SeaWorld uses to describe its amusement park to the four million customers who visited the year we found JJ. Most came to see the killer whale, synchronized swimming dolphins, and sea otters rescued from the oil of the Exxon Valdez in Alaska. SeaWorld's public has long been conflicted about these marine mammals however—enthusiastic public support for some kind of environmental protection led to the passage of landmark legislation in the early 1970s, but that same public swelled SeaWorld's coffers when they first unveiled Gigi and killer whales in captivity.

Neither public opinion nor the 1972 Marine Mammal Protection Act, which SeaWorld called "anti-zoo, irrational, needless over-regulation," slowed the hunting of sea creatures in the wild. SeaWorld tried to capture more orcas in Puget Sound in 1976 under the new system of federal permits, but violated the conditions that such captures be done humanely. The state of Washington sued.

"We reached settlement only after testimony began to come into the courtroom in the trial about previous captures where lots of whales had died," said former Washington Secretary of State Ralph Munro. "And obviously, SeaWorld did not want these things revealed. They wanted to keep them hidden and they did not want to own up to the fact that they'd killed a lot of whales in the capture process."

Peter Wallerstein had campaigned against the captive marine mammal industry for years as a part of his work to rescue and protect these creatures. He put himself between boats chartered by the Shedd Aquarium in Chicago and the Pacific white-sided dolphins they aimed to capture, only to watch as these NMFS-authorized hunts injured dozens of animals to capture three—one of which died within weeks. He uncovered video footage of SeaWorld executives overseeing bloody whale and dolphin "drive hunts" in Japan at the same time they gave interviews saying they had no part in such practices.

"I mean, Jacques Cousteau and documentaries and even Marlin Perkins, I remember as a kid I couldn't wait for the next Jacques Cousteau film…I was inspired by film," Peter reminisced, outlining his alternative to the captive displays. "I don't think I saw a real whale until I was probably an adult…so I don't buy the whole captive display industries or the zoo industries saying that you need to touch, you need to hear, you need to see in person to have appreciation for these animals…I don't buy that…I don't buy that!"

Like the Shedd aquarium, SeaWorld kept many of its practices secret, in part to avoid public outrage and in part to circumvent the law. Although there was nothing illegal about capturing whales in Japan or Iceland, Peter discovered that SeaWorld claimed that some of the whales caught under their direct supervision were already in captivity to circumvent US prohibition of the import of wild specimens. John Hall, the former SeaWorld Research Director, revealed that SeaWorld chief veterinarian Dr. Lanny Cornell personally micro-managed the hunt, capture, storage, and transfer of whales, but ordered all traces of his employer to be eliminated from boats and capture gear, later telling Hall "You didn't see any of this. You didn't hear any of this. You weren't here."

"The price paid by wild animals is not limited to those collected and taken to places like SeaWorld," Peter reminded me as we debated if we should now ask for the theme park's help. "The barbarity of drive hunts, the decimation of whale and dolphin family groups that are known to divide labor and societal duties in sophisticated, inter-dependent ways, means that larger populations are left vulnerable and helpless, just so that one of their number might supposedly "educate" the humans."

Volumes have been written, debated, filmed, and photographed about these practices, especially the drive hunts in Japan, but author and naturalist Sakae Hemmi of the non-profit Whale and Dolphin Conservation Society, distills it simply after thirty years of research and campaigning.

"If dolphins could speak…one of them kept in an aquarium… might say, "My family lived in the ocean, freely swimming around. One day, all of a sudden, we were chased by fishing boats, threatened by noises from the banging of metal pipes, driven to a shallow inlet and confined there. My father died from suffocation after becoming entangled in fishing nets. My mother was slaughtered with a knife for human consumption. My sister died of shock when she was lifted out of the water and my brother drowned during the capture procedure. Both of them were processed for meat and eaten by humans and their pets. I myself survived, was brought into this aquarium, taught tricks, and am working to entertain you."

In the end, public outrage against videos of bloody drive hunts and first-hand testimony of former employees was so virulent that SeaWorld ended these efforts and changed tactics. Like Japanese whalers today, "science" would become the justification used by SeaWorld for the capture and exploitation of marine mammals for profit. They partnered with a small research organization to create the Hubbs-SeaWorld Research Institute, initially funded by other industries—real estate developers looking for ways to justify the destruction of least tern coastal nesting sites and the US Navy trying to justify underwater explosions despite the apparent harm to whales. SeaWorld also used the institute to justify its exploitation of marine mammals, often citing its findings as if they came from independent academia.

To improve the appearance of SeaWorld as a place of learning, park designers methodically eliminated human elements from the orca show to make it appear more "natural"—Shamu ditched the sunglasses, for example, and followed jets of water around the theatre-pool instead of a ball and stick. But the inmates didn't always cooperate with the jailers. In 1987 an orca almost killed a trainer, which resulted in revelations about many similar incidents, including one at another theme park where the trainer was killed. In 1989 two orcas died mysteriously, including one mother orca bleeding to death in front of park visitors. Although different animals played Shamu to ensure a steady stream of consistent performances, the orcas were often bored and reluctant to perform. Trainers improvised each show, often skipping over tricks that the whales refused to do. When it couldn't be hidden from the crowd in the bleachers, the trainers would simply start rattling off facts about whales as filler.

To further camouflage the reluctance of the whales to stick to the human script, SeaWorld shows began to use musical scores, like a movie, to enhance public emotion and the sense of entertainment. Sea lions were given more duties in longer shows programmed around the shorter more-hyped orca shows. SeaWorld conscripted dozens of interchangeable sea lion "Clydes" and "Seamores," that reproduce easily in captivity and are far cheaper to maintain, performing more frequently in smaller venues around the park to give the sense of something always going on.

This may all seem like a lot of trouble for an amusement park that is equal measures of zoo and shopping mall, but despite claims of science, research, and some legitimate rehabilitation, SeaWorld and its kind exist to make money—money for a lot of people in a very long supply chain, from fishermen in poor island nations who catch whales and dolphins to the Cuban and Russian governments that derive significant foreign currency from selling the animals. Dolphins captured in the 1960s sold for $300, but today command over $100,000 each. One Mexican swim-with-the-dolphins company claimed it could sell a dolphin calf for $400,000, which may not be surprising given that a similar facility in Florida earns over $500 million each year. In the 1990s, SeaWorld bought a killer whale for $875,000, but today they are worth up to $5 million and are used as collateral for loans. Even when they die, decades earlier than they would in the wild, they are worth a fortune—their owners reap payouts from million-dollar life insurance policies.

"If you wanted a strong cash flow to continue, you needed a steady supply of killer whales, especially if you're expanding and building new parks," said John Hall, the former Director of Research for SeaWorld, who estimates that seventy percent of every dollar earned at SeaWorld comes from the presence of killer whales. "You need whales to fill them up."

To its credit, SeaWorld does contribute a portion of ticket sales to support wildlife conservation, including protecting tigers from poaching in India and a million dollars a year to support a network of small facilities and personnel to rescue small marine mammals and birds. But do those dollars offset the damage done to wild populations? Or offset the inhumane treatment of the individuals that are conscripted to perform and die prematurely in cramped concrete enclosures?

Is there a sufficient educational benefit to outweigh the obvious impacts to captive marine mammals? An objective review of the body of scientific research from marine theme parks could easily conclude that, while there is certainly some motivational education of the public and contribution to conservation and environmental protection, the claims of scientific research benefits are largely without merit. The underlying question then boils down to ethics—do we have the right to harm individual marine mammals and the societal groups they are removed from, for our own financial benefit and limited educational value?

All of this made a rescue of JJ by SeaWorld tantalizing but risky for all concerned—she might never do tricks or respond to movie music, but people might pay money to see an orphan rehabilitated and returned to the wild. Yet we were now in the position of asking SeaWorld to use its resources to help JJ, indeed willing to trade her freedom—and whatever fate Nature would impose upon her—for her survival in captivity, at least for several months. If SeaWorld agreed, how could we argue with the way they make the profits that allow them to support such a project? And wouldn't the public benefit, both scientifically and emotionally, by seeing JJ grow to maturity and be released back into the wild?

"Tough one, but I would say no," Kris Haddad said over the radio as we added her to our debate. "Personally, until the day with JJ, I had never seen a whale up close or been to a SeaWorld kind of place so my only connection was through photos and documentaries. That was enough to make me love them. I went to plenty of zoos as a child and always loved it, but I don't think I understood that the animals were out of their natural habitat and were suffering. I now realize that these animals are literally being held captive and are torn away from their families. The research that is done on whales in captivity is not accurate, in so much as it's research that is being done on a whale in captivity not in the wild."

She was right. Ironically, despite the value to the box office of captive marine mammals, there seems to be a "disposable" approach to their care. A pregnant sea lion at one aquarium in California jumped to her death in front of workers who were cleaning her enclosure and had not moved her to a safer location. Chlorine in tanks at a Florida aquarium was so high that dolphins couldn't open their eyes and their skin peeled. Eye blisters developed on a sea lion at a North Carolina pool because it had no shade. A dolphin died after swallowing coins thrown into her tank in Kentucky and another died after eating sunglasses and car keys. Dozens more have died across the country from ham-fisted medical attention and anesthesia. Of the fifteen hundred deaths reported to authorities in one recent ten year period alone, hundreds were from completely preventable causes, while the captive marine mammal display industry—led by SeaWorld—successfully lobbied the federal government for less oversight and reporting of these incidents.

Suppressing regulation has not changed the facts however. A year before we met JJ, a review of five thousand captive animals in one hundred ninety facilities revealed that most were taken from the wild and that the majority died within two years, despite the fact that only the youngest, strongest specimens are captured in the first place. Orcas typically live to sixty years, but no captive had ever passed twenty. The world's most famous orca may provide an illustrative example of this "disposable" approach to marine mammal care.

That orca was named Keiko, the star of the movie Free Willy, held in a marine park in Mexico City for a decade in a tank that was only five times his body length. In Nature, he would live in a world with virtually no boundaries, an ocean realm of more than three hundred million cubic miles. He was fed dead, headless tropical fish, instead of hunting live food, as he would have done in the waters of his native Iceland. With a poor substitute diet, nothing to do, and very little room to swim, he lolled listlessly and wore down his teeth from gnawing at the cement sides of his tank. He became anemic, developed ulcers and swallowed floats, balls, and metal objects out of boredom. The overheated water, compared to the crisp sea around Iceland, resulted in skin lesions and the thin, dry air "scorched" Keiko's lungs. Think about it—no whale has ever taken a breath at anything except sea level, but this air was at an altitude of seventy four hundred feet and contained just one percent water vapor. Moreover, the air quality in Mexico City is notoriously among the world's worst, meaning Keiko was as susceptible to asthma and reduced lung function as any human suffering from those diseases in the city.

Keiko shut down his sonar, because when he clicked, nothing came back and nothing ever changed. Humans hear passively—whatever sound arrives at the ear—but whales listen actively, sending out clicks and gauging their world by what comes back. Keiko had simply given up.

Public outcry, over media reports on the fate of the real "Willy," led to action by the film's producers and philanthropists, who ultimately rehabilitated the whale and released him in his native waters off of Iceland. Despite more than a year of unprecedented and costly efforts to repatriate Keiko to passing pods of orcas, he died from a sudden onset of pneumonia.

"Marine mammals were an expendable commodity," said Jim Antrim, Vice President of Zoological Operations at SeaWorld. "If these animals perished, you'd just go out and replace them. The ease [of replacing them] didn't drive a great deal of research of what they needed to keep them healthy."

To his credit, when Antrim got the call about JJ he told local officials that he was constrained by NMFS and Joe Cordaro. As long as the animal was uninjured and swimming freely, the NMFS protocol was to wait twenty four hours to see if the animal would "repatriate" with its kin. Antrim was on his way to a conference in Houston, Texas, that morning and told officials to keep him posted in case things changed. Based on the experience with Gigi, Antrim estimated that a rescue and rehabilitation of another whale calf would need at least a million dollars and could end in an embarrassing public failure if JJ died. He suspected his superiors would never go along with such a risk.

John Heyning of the Los Angeles Natural History Museum, one of the officials that Antrim received first-hand accounts of JJ's condition from, told Peter bluntly that SeaWorld would not soon be coming to the rescue. Heyning may have helped to dissuade Antrim from taking action, because he was now waiting on the beach, with a specially-designed flatbed truck and a very different agenda—he hoped to take away what he assumed would soon be a carcass for dissection and study in his lab.

Slender, blond, 40-ish, and mustachioed, with a vague resemblance to Shakespearean actor Kenneth Branagh, Heyning used his flatbed to haul dozens of dead marine mammals from California beaches every year, adding to the scientific literature about dolphins and whales by studying what he collected. But there was something vulture-ish about him sitting on the beach predicting when JJ would succumb and glancing at his watch as if he hoped to get her body back to the museum before some hot Friday night date. We'll never know if he encouraged Antrim to help with a rescue instead, but he certainly displayed no interest in that course of action when asked by reporters.

While some were waiting for JJ to die, the bond with her only grew stronger for Peter and me. Considering what it took to bring her into the world, ending her life in the drab waters of a man-made boat harbor seemed more cruel than the life she would face in a tank in captivity.

Although we didn't want to contemplate her death here, we knew that her birth in these waters would have been brief and dramatic. Probably the day before, two days at most, Marina would have raised her tail above the surface and slowly lowered it several times in a span of less than ten minutes, at which point JJ emerged tail first underwater, flukes folded to her chest. The short, rigid umbilical cord would have broken easily and the dark pink newborn would have popped to the surface for its first breath of air. Seagulls would have descended to eat the afterbirth as JJ's flaccid and rubbery flukes attempted a rudimentary dog paddle around her mother.

Within hours, JJ would have been swimming with some skill along Marina's midsection, where a draft helped her along like a car following bumper to bumper behind the leader in a race. Gradually testing deeper waters, then jumping on Marina's back and sliding off in play like a puppy, she probably paused periodically to nurse, the thick, fatty mother's milk sticking quickly to her massive tongue, always communicating with her mother by a series of low rumbling and metallic steel-drum sounds and clicks—a language learned from mother to calf and now heard by the two humans who were trying to save her life, but who were clueless about how to respond.

Oddly, it was her tongue that John Heyning coveted the most. Some years earlier, his research in New Zealand led him to believe that grays manipulate their body temperature, from the tepid waters of Mexico to the crisp environment of the Arctic, by using their plus-sized tongues as heat exchangers. Heyning became obsessed with proving his theory and had harvested dozens of tongues from stranded whales, discovering arteries and tissue that could only be explained by his thesis. Ironically, given his deathwatch now for JJ, he lacked the final evidence for proving his theory that could only be obtained from a living specimen.

"We lacked the physiological proof that they actually worked to conserve body heat in gray whales," he said with energetic scientific curiosity. "And proof seemed impossible to get – no baleen whales were held in captivity and free-swimming gray whales were not likely to have much interest in allowing us to take temperature readings from inside of their mouths."

JJ could be that opportunity, if she could be saved instead of simply becoming another harvested specimen. But Heyning maintained a scientific detachment, waiting, much like Joe Cordaro at NMFS, for Nature to decide the matter and in the process dictate his own fate too.

Peter, Kris, and I had made up our minds. We would advocate for her rescue and rehabilitation, knowing that she would outgrow any facility that even SeaWorld could maintain and that if she survived, she had a chance to be returned to the wild. As darkness fell, we knew that only a press onslaught would motivate SeaWorld, so we began dialing every reporter within a hundred miles.

Many of the Native American tribes along the Pacific coast believe we are related to whales and dolphins. We began a campaign to save a family member. Kris called every reporter we knew and hunted down the ones around the marina looking for information about the orphaned whale.

"I think in the past you could say that Nature has led to the extinction of animals, however now I believe most animals are becoming extinct as a result of human activity," Kris told a reporter who asked if we were interfering with Mother Nature. "We are, in so many cases, responsible for extinction, while in the past it was a natural occurrence, part of the evolutionary process. One could argue however that it's part of the evolutionary process that man became dominant and through his dominance has caused extinctions. But all of that said, I think that any time we can rescue a living creature we should feel compelled to do so. We are all linked together. In doing so, we exhibit our humanity and our connection to our brothers and sisters of the sea."

Kris also called dozens of BayKeeper volunteers and asked them to flood TV stations, SeaWorld, and Cordaro's line at NMFS with calls demanding that JJ be rescued. Beverly called and emailed her friends and the philanthropic employees behind her foundation and suggested similar action. We had no idea if anyone was listening, in a world of MTV-length attention spans and a theatrical trial of an aging football player that dominated the nightly news, but we had to try.

We had to try, whether or not JJ was our sister in a literal sense, because our lives had been spent trying to rescue the ocean from human ignorance and waste. Now, if we couldn't help even this one creature that the sea had delivered into our care, what hope was there for restoring the entire ocean to its former health? Kris, Peter, Beverly, David, and I had not said it in so many words, but for each of us, this was not just a moment of fact in our lives, it was a moment of faith.

Chapter 4

NIGHTFALL

There's not much light to lose on a gray January day, but as the last few shreds of it dissolved in the late afternoon, JJ's strength seemed to evaporate in equal measure. She had stopped "playing" a few hours earlier, no longer testing our boats and trying to lift her various body parts out of the water. Her trips between my boat and Peter's took longer each time and she lingered a few feet away instead of vigorously searching our hulls for a nipple. She stopped altogether the bewitching practice of rolling to one side to make eye contact with her human companions.

Was this the beginning of the end? Weakened by hunger and disoriented by our inability to connect her to another whale, was she now going to let Nature consign her to organic oblivion? Or was this the gray whale version of an afternoon nap, timed perfectly with natural rhythms of the fading light?

Darkness falls in southern California's mid-winter by about 5 P.M. and, although there was still much of Friday left, it seemed as if some kind of end had already arrived when the ship's clock on my boat struck two bells—five o'clock. From one boat to the other, we exchanged concerns, but neither of us could say for certain what was happening, nor make predictions with any accuracy.

Bop...bop...

bop-bop-bop…
bop-bop…
Pause.
Repeat.

It may have been our heightened sense of hearing in the advancing darkness, but we thought we heard JJ croaking in a pattern we had not noticed before, something akin to a bongo played softly on the other side of a wall, interspersed with croaks more like someone running a thumb over a washboard.

Bop…
bop…
bop-bop-bop…
bop-bop.
Pause.
Repeat.

Was she asking or telling? Was she expecting a reply? JJ spent more time underwater between each visit to one of our boats, another cause for some concern. Gray whales store over forty percent of their oxygen in muscles compared to humans, who store just thirteen percent, allowing them to take three or four breaths at the surface and stay below for a quarter of an hour or longer. Their lungs take twice the oxygen from the air as we do, in part because they exhale ninety percent of the oxygen-depleted air—we expel just fifteen percent every time we exhale—giving them still more ability to hold each breath they take. Although we couldn't know how efficient JJ's cardiovascular system had become at such an early age, her parents had hearts that weigh nearly three hundred pounds and that could slow to half their normal rate when diving—from ten beats a minute to five—to preserve oxygen. Did JJ already possess some of those skills or was her strength fading and she was slowly drowning beneath the now-black waters of the bay?

"The breath of the whale is frequently attended with such an insupportable smell, as to bring on a disorder of the brain," Melville says in Moby Dick. But each time JJ returned to our vicinity and exhaled in a shower of spray and whooshing sounds, we quietly rejoiced.

Those sounds and smells grew more important to us as we carefully shifted our boats to keep track of her, because the pitch black of night, punctuated only by reflections of shore-based lights shattered by the wind-whipped waves, made sightings of her all but impossible. On the other hand, because our boats were illuminated by colorful running lights, was JJ looking at us?

If she was, what did she actually see? Her eyes were encapsulated in a thick fibrous cocoon to protect them from pressure at depth, adapted for seeing in the dark ocean with extra wide pupils, constructed to perceive things as smaller than they really are—one of the planet's largest creatures, already dwarfing most other living things, perceiving them as smaller still. In humans, the area of the brain for sight and sound are about equal. Perhaps because sound travels five times faster in the ocean than in the air and thousands of miles farther, the sound area of the brain in gray whales is much larger than the area applied to sight, suggesting that sound is the more important sense.

Bop...

bop...

bop-bop-bop...

bop-bop.

Pause.

Repeat.

As Peter and I tried to decipher her sounds the dark, the cold and drizzle made our own situation seem ever gloomier. Neither of us had planned for a night on the water, each of us now wrapped in an odd array of windbreakers, blankets, life jackets, and plastic tarps. Anything to push back the mist and trap precious warmth near the body. Our focus on an animal in the water led us to pass the time talking about other creatures in our lives.

"And she just caught my eye, shivering in her little cage." Peter said of a mutt he spied in a local animal shelter as we chattered haphazardly to fill the time between JJ sightings. "I asked what was her problem and they said...'well, she's got about thirty minutes, we got to put her down'...the City of LA gives strays just forty-eight hours to live and then kills them...and she was on that list...one of my problems, a personal thing, I empathize too well with animals…so I'm in that cage with her…I'm the sea lion with a gillnet on it, I'm the animals suffering in captivity or being captured and being taken away from their family." He adopted the mutt and cried that he couldn't take them all.

"Peter, what do you remember as a kid was your first image of a whale," I asked. "Pinocchio or Jonah getting swallowed by a whale? Moby Dick?"

"Moby Dick for me, I don't know how I felt as a kid but now it's a triumph of the whale because Moby Dick survived," Peter laughed. "Yeah, Moby Dick took that fuckin' Ahab and took him down…so to me Moby Dick is a great image, it brings good things in my head, the survival of the great whale, and a little payback too…Free Willy too, I wished they were all free…I mean, that movie did bring a lot of attention and it really put us forward many years as far as getting the word out about the plight of captive whales…and even though it was a Hollywood production, it still worked…and the bottom line is Willy is free right now, right?"

Keiko, the whale used in the film, had indeed been set free because of media attention. We needed the same media motivation to free JJ in another sense, to force SeaWorld to try and rehabilitate her and save her from starvation and drowning, assuming it wasn't already too late. The local media was now doing live broadcasts for the evening news, some picked up by national and foreign stations. SeaWorld began receiving calls—hundreds of them—from concerned kids around the globe begging for the rescue of JJ.

Earnest and fit in middle age, boyish with a bowl-cut head of short salt-and-pepper hair, Jim Antrim sat in his Houston hotel room knowing that the media din would grow louder and that he needed to prepare his bosses with a good answer. SeaWorld was owned by beer giant Anheuser-Busch, so he called his corporate superior and was amazed when he was given the green light to spend the money—if NMFS gave its permission to attempt a rescue in the first place. Antrim called Heyning to relay the news, but made it clear that SeaWorld would not act without federal authority and only if someone else delivered the whale to the park in San Diego.

Even as the drumbeat for a solution grew louder, our hopes for JJ waned. By 9 P.M. on Friday night, neither of us had seen nor heard her for more than an hour. She might simply have moved off to another part of the marina, the bay, or even the mouth of adjacent Ballona Creek, but for all we knew, she might be drifting lifeless back out to sea. Peter needed food and fuel, so he returned to the dock while I kept the watch, but I was soon joined by a local charter boat skippered by Bertram McCann.

Bertram spent most of his time handling yachts for wealthy clients and renting out barges and support boats for moviemakers. Hollywood has long been fascinated by whales, from Moby Dick to Free Willy to Star Trek IV, but these were not the first storytellers to fall under the spell of whales.

The Haida people of the Pacific Northwest believe orcas are humans lost at sea, just as the Chumash people of central California see dolphins as human brothers and sisters. Farther south, thousand year old petroglyphs around San Ignacio Lagoon in central Baja speak to ancient relations between man and whale—sketches on rocks of sloping humps, knuckled backs, and water spouting high above. Some thought they had telepathic connection to whales and shared a rich, interdependent cultural life.

To be sure, native peoples have also depended on the majesty of gray whales not only for inspiration in art, but also for their own survival. Aleut people in Alaska haven't hunted gray whales for hundreds of years, but certainly took advantage of whales that came ashore, while neighboring Alutiiq people hunted regularly for meat with strict cultural ceremony, using poison-tipped darts, sometimes in the hands of solo hunters proving themselves in elaborate rites of passage. Hunters would live apart before the hunt like shamans with cleansing, chants, and sleepless nights, in regalia resembling the orca or gray whale. Once hunted and killed, long incantations to spirits helped bring the bounty ashore. Grateful tribespeople honored the animal and the hunter with dances five times around a fire and the roasting meat, its spirit carried to the heavens on the smoke.

If JJ were to survive, modern media, not petroglyphs or smoke signals, would have to persuade federal officials and SeaWorld executives to help. As Bertram and I slowly circled the nearshore area in our boats, listening and drifting, sweeping the waves with searchlights, hoping, fearful, and cold, "Earthman" David Garcia stood on the rock jetty with his news camera lights glaring. David told the story, eloquently, compellingly, with live-or-die simplicity. By the 10 P.M. news, it was the top story and the calls to SeaWorld clogged the automatic switchboard. The response clearly had struck a chord with people of every age and background.

As we circled in the water behind David's position looking for JJ, I found myself chanting softly, to stay awake and perhaps to channel some native spirit helper. I whispered the Latin name for gray whales, "eschrichtius robustus," aloud over and over.

"Eshhh—rick—tee—us...Row—bust—us." Brothers and sisters, warm-blooded analogs, sentient communicators that need no spoken language when their eye meets ours. Whatever they are called and whatever the connection between humans and whales, whether JJ was still in the area or not, Bertram and I were definitely not alone—millions were inspired to hang on David's telling of JJ's story and to protest any thought of watching her perish.

"Eshhh—rick—tee—us...Row—bust—us. Eshhh—rick—tee—us...Row—bust—us." With nothing to do but stand by, it was hard to stay awake, no matter what I did or said, and regardless of Native American beliefs or human good wishes that night, JJ's fate might already have been decided. By midnight, we had not seen her for nearly four hours. Bertram headed back to the marina. The bay was empty of human life, save for me in the BayKeeper patrol boat, drifting in silence and straining to hear any evidence that JJ was spending this night with me.

"Eshhh—rick—tee—us...Row—bust—us. Eshhh—rick—tee—us...Row—bust—us."

The fog had finally cleared to reveal a moonless night and a handful of stars that shone through the light pollution from the City of Angels. With little to retain any warmth and a strengthening breeze, as six bells struck on the ship's clock at 3 A.M., I found myself doing jumping jacks on the deck to keep from shivering. The cold made it seem even more hopeless that JJ had survived the night.

Grays are voluntary breathers, thinking purposefully each time they inhale. If JJ was just asleep, her first full night of life outside the womb, half of her brain would be shut down and sleeping, the other half alert and focused on breathing. She might be mostly below the surface, breathing quietly through her blowhole or, as grays are known to do, she might be lying on the bottom of the sea, surfacing slowly now and then to breathe. Her heartbeat would be slowed, one eye closed and the other open, her body might twitch from time to time, a sign she was in a deeper state of sleep, dreaming like other mammals. This night, thousands of humans had seen David's reporting, images of a baby gray whale, and were dreaming of her. Was she dreaming of us?

"Eshhh—rick—tee—us…Row—bust—us. Eshhh—rick—tee—us…Row—bust—us."

"BayKeeper One…BayKeeper One…come in please, this is BayKeeper base," the patrol boat radio crackled, somewhere around 6 A.M., startling me from my chanting stupor.

"Ah…go ahead BayKeeper base…this is BayKeeper One," I replied hazily.

"There may be a chink in the SeaWorld armor and they may be open to a rescue after all," Kris reported eagerly, having just heard the news from Antrim and Heyning. "So do you think we can get NMFS to say yes? And if he does, just how would we get JJ more than a hundred miles down the coast?"

"Stand by, BayKeeper One," I said, over a massive yawn. "That's good news…but right now we don't have a whale to bring them."

Chapter 5

TWO HUNDRED HANDS

Weather can make a mood, but it also has the power to mock. On the day we discovered JJ, no amount of cold fog could chill our hopeful energy, our sense that her story would end happily. As Saturday morning dawned, clear and blindingly bright blue, no amount of sunshine could chase the sense of failure. We had not seen JJ for the past dozen hours.

Whether SeaWorld had succumbed to withering pressure from the press and public, saw a potentially profitable new attraction, or wanted to use its considerable resources to attempt a good karmic deed, Antrim had indeed sent the message that he would take the baby gray whale—if we could deliver her to their door a hundred twenty miles away. It was no small task to consider, but before we could even do that, we still needed the approval of Joe Cordaro at the National Marine Fisheries Service. Oh, and there was the small matter that as the sun rose fully over the horizon, we had no whale in sight to rescue.

"When they saw her thrashing in the shallows off the California coast, everyone knew this baby gray whale was in trouble," read the full-page ad that SeaWorld later placed in major magazines under the headline, "What do you need to rescue a 1600 pound baby? Just a few days old, with her umbilical cord still attached, she had somehow lost her mother, and almost any chance of survival. SeaWorld volunteered to help."

I had motored back to the BayKeeper headquarters for a thermos of coffee and a fresh bagel that Kris had magically made appear in our galley, knowing there might be a few volunteers to feed. I gave her the sober update on our lost orphan and she cheerfully offered several explanations for the disappearance that might still result in a happy ending. Neither of us really bought it though.

"Fifty-eight messages on this damn machine," she cursed, rolling her eyes and putting a parka over her sweater. Kris was always cold. "We both have our work cut out. I'll stick by the radio…in case…"

Her words trailed off as she started pressing buttons and listening to recorded offers to help, reports on the "pressure SeaWorld" campaign from volunteers, random questions ("are gray whales meat eaters?"), and several reporters needing an update. We agreed not to call the reporters back yet.

By first light, I aimed the patrol boat back out to sea, hoping to catch sight of JJ, alive or dead. I patrolled the marina first, in case she had taken refuge in shallower waters, then slowly glided along the main channel, expecting to see her surface and blow a spray of seawater into the morning air. Where the main channel from the marina empties into the sea, I turned left, towards Ballona Creek, the mouth of the massive stormdrain on the south side of the rock jetty. After a quick circle or two, slugging the coffee that now had cooled in the big tip-proof ceramic mug, I decided to look on the seaward side of the breakwater a hundred yards to the west.

Before my hand hit the throttle, I felt something bump the boat. Was I too close to the jetty that separates Ballona Creek from the marina? Did I hit a submerged rock?

If I had hit a rock, it was one that could breathe—because I heard a sudden whoosh of water and air.

There she was, on the starboard side of the boat, looking for a nipple, exhaling vigorously as she came to the surface. She nudged the hull and rolled over to make eye contact. I had no way of knowing if she felt some relief, pleasure, or kinship at reuniting with my boat, but

I certainly felt elated to see her. I reached cautiously toward her, stroking her and muttering something that was probably irrelevant to her, but which made me feel soothed, and wondered how hungry and tired she must be.

JJ raised her tail out of the water and slapped it with infantile authority. Was she demanding food, playing, or struggling? I watched her movements around the boat, trying to glean whether her health was stable or declining, what our chances were of getting her to SeaWorld before she starved to death, as I radioed for Peter to give him the news.

"That's amazing, 'cause I thought you were calling to say you found her floating belly-up in the Creek," Peter's voice crackled back on the radio. "I'm launching now—see you in ten."

As I waved a curious fishing boat away, I saw a plastic lawn chair floating down Ballona Creek a few yards away. Once a natural stream, Ballona Creek had been channelized with concrete decades ago to prevent flooding and to drain the massive annual rainstorms that pummel Los Angeles. Although very efficient at moving rain water from the land to the sea, the concrete creek was also very effective at delivering tons of pollution along with it, washed from streets via thousands of storm drains.

The green plastic chair, one leg missing, instantly gave me the answer to the question Peter and I debated yesterday. Why rescue an animal that Nature has chosen to eliminate from the gene pool? In short, because humans have so assaulted the ocean, and the creatures in it, that we cannot afford to pass up any opportunity to give something back. Given the scope of the damage, in such a relatively short period of time, we may also be the reason that Marina abandoned her newborn.

But therein lies an irony. So many people had rallied to persuade SeaWorld to attempt the rescue of one, when their collective actions threaten the very existence of many. Three quarters of the world's fish stocks have been fished out of commercial existence, while trawlers scrape the bottom of the sea to find more, destroying the ability of the ocean to help those species recover. Even derelict fishing gear—lost nets, like the ones that entangled the first whale that Peter

Figure 11: *Urban Stormwater runoff Ballona Creek*

rescued, and miles of abandoned "longlines," studded with hundreds of hooks—becomes silent, unintended death traps for fish, birds, and marine mammals.

Greenhouse gases from burning fossil fuels, a third of which are absorbed by the ocean, have changed the chemistry of the sea, bleaching every coral reef on earth, in some cases resulting in their complete destruction, while plankton and other food at the base of the web of life literally dissolve.

Vast garbage patches, the size of Texas, comprised largely of plastic debris, slowly drift in immortal circles in a dozen oceans around the globe.

The equivalent of ten Exxon Valdez oil spills happen each year at sea, fed by leaking pipes, ships, drilling rigs, and stormwater runoff that is polluted by the excrement of our cars, a death of a trillion cuts.

The ocean's nursery, wetlands and mangroves, have been drained and scraped clean by coastal development, over ninety percent paved over in many sensitive coastline habitats around the world, including southern California.

When it rains, even waste from domestic cats is carried into the surf, transmitting feline diseases to sea otters, not unlike the diseases that white settlers transmitted to Indian tribes, whose immune systems could not resist, killing them in genocidal numbers.

And beyond these unfathomable, mostly invisible injuries to the sea, three more human-made insults may pose the greatest risk to the long-term survival of JJ and other whales. Sound pollution, chemical toxins, and whaling.

One spring day in Washington State in 2003, whale researcher Ken Balcom was observing orcas in Puget Sound. His monitoring equipment recorded underwater sonic "booms" made by US Navy vessels, along with sounds from whales he had never heard before— the orcas were literally screaming in fear and pain. Porpoises fled the area; orcas swam to shore; others struggled to poke their heads above water to flee the noise.

Although he had never heard such vocal anguish from whales, Ken was not new to the issue of high-powered Navy sonar tests. Three years earlier an orca suddenly beached itself in front of his house. Then seventeen more orcas, a dolphin and two minke whales followed suit. At least six later died and, when Ken scanned Puget Sound for a source, he spotted a US Navy destroyer doing sonar exercises with a battle group.

"All these creatures we had spent ten years studying were dying… in front of our eyes," Ken recalls with sadness and anger. "Any whale within fifty miles suffers."

Ken collected two heads among the dead whales and took them to Harvard for CT scans. The brains and ears had suffered massive internal hemorrhaging and bleeding. The pain must have been excruciating. Science can't tell us if those impacts are from human-made underwater sonic booms or, frightened by the sounds, if the animals rush to the surface and suffer pressure-related injuries, just as a human would experience from surfacing too quickly after diving. Either way, whales are not that much different from humans when faced with fearful explosions, both in terms of the natural reaction to fear and the physiological results.

Whales are more at risk than we are, because of the medium in which they live. The ocean is so much more dense than air, so sound travels faster and farther. Sound waves also travel through fat with alarming force. Some whales and dolphins have fat-filled cavities in the head to absorb normal sounds to help them echo-locate or navigate—making them up to ten times more sensitive than humans—but when intensely loud sound hits those cavities, they are injured or simply explode.

Even small injury to a whale's hearing can be life-threatening, because they rely on sound for so many aspects of survival in the wild. Their clicks are sonic signals, like those used by submarines, and the sound wave bouncing off of food, obstacles, predators, or each other returns to their "ears" with vital information for survival and socialization.

We have known that our acoustic pollution harms whales for more than a century. Whalers in the 1850s and scientists a hundred thirty years later both observed that noise drives whales away, especially mothers and calves. Even non-lethal sounds can interfere with a whale's life—the acoustic traffic jam we create, composed of Navy weapons, supertankers whose props emit a low-frequency hiss, explosions for oil exploration, and seismic survey air guns. Even our research into climate change has hurt whales—high-intensity, low frequency sound waves are used to measure the speed of sound, which can determine changing sea temperature and salinity.

If JJ survived and was one day returned to her natural migration path along the west coast of North America, she would not only be assaulted by inescapable noise, but by equally inescapable toxins in her food and ocean environment. Washington State expects about four stranded or dead whales in a year, typically from old age and normal disease or predation, but in 1999 and 2000, those deaths increased six-fold. Scientists found them all starving, likely due to pollution and climate change-induced food shortages. The dead whales had high levels of human-made chemicals like PCBs in their tissues, but researchers believe toxic industrial waste and polluted runoff may have killed the amphipods, fish and crab larvae, and shrimp they eat from the sediments, resulting in their emaciation and starvation.

"The ocean is downhill of everything on earth, and the result is that everything flows into the ocean from higher ground, and that means it's the ultimate cesspool basically of the world," says Roger Payne, who discovered that whales sing and recorded them for National Geographic a generation ago, and who now spends his days testing whales for toxins. "All sorts of things, including synthetic molecules [from which] human beings make a huge variety of different things. We're concerned about things like fire retardants [and] things like mercury and other metals and persistent organic pollutants, which is a category so large as to be almost useless, but nevertheless a whole series of molecules which we're looking at a few of. Many of the substances that we're concerned with are fantastically insoluble in water. They are highly soluble in fat. So what happens is that they end up in the ocean water, anywhere in parts per trillion or parts per quadrillion, so hugely diluted. But as soon as they get into fats they end up in very, very high concentrations because the fats can hold lots of them. The trouble is the animals don't have any way of dealing with them so they store them, and then they get passed on when some other animal eats that animal. So here on your plate is a pound of swordfish. It took a million pounds of diatoms to create that one pound—not the whole fish—just that one pound. A million pounds is five hundred tons, so it took fifty, ten-ton truckloads of diatoms to make that one pound of swordfish. So you take all those trucks and you park them along a row, it's about ten blocks long, and to the end of that row you attach your liver and with it you detoxify that entire line of trucks. And that's what you do when you eat a pound of swordfish."

Whales are just like swordfish when it comes to storing most toxins, and dying from them, but there may be an ironic benefit from at least one potent toxin in the ocean—mercury. Most of the mercury in the sea comes from coal-fired powerplant smokestacks and oil drilling rigs, but as a result of the processes Payne describes as "bioaccumulation in fat, along with biomagnification, that occurs when contaminated animals are eaten by other animals, effectively concentrating the vast pool of pollution," dolphins have become so toxic that they can no longer be consumed by humans. Every winter, Japanese whalers in Taiji drive whales and dolphins into a secluded bay and club them to death, turning the shallow waters red, selling the meat to markets and fertilizer manufacturers. But recent testing shows the meat is too toxic for either purpose, dealing what may be a fatal blow to this barbaric Japanese hunting practice.

The Taiji "drive hunt" is just one example of the third major human impact on whales, one that many people assume ended with the advent of the modern conservation movement in the 1970s—whaling.

"I'll chase him round Good Hope, and round the Horn, and round the Norway Maelstrom, and round perdition's flames before I give him up," proclaims Captain Ahab, speaking of the great white whale in Herman Melville's classic tale of both American whaling and human obsession, Moby Dick. Writing just before the Civil War, Melville enshrined fear of whales that persisted for generations

"…the half-foundered ship with its three dismantled masts alone visible; and an exasperated whale, purposing to spring clean over the craft…" he wrote. He also described actual monuments to lost whalers in New England bearing sentiments like "to the memory of the crew of the Eliza who were towed out of sight by a whale" and "to the memory of Captain Hardy, who in the bows of his boat was killed by a sperm whale on the coast of Japan." Inspired by the true story of a real sperm whale, is it any wonder that popular culture of the day vilified the great beasts? "Mocha Dick," as he was called, patrolled the south Atlantic to the waters off Japan, and in more than a hundred fights with whalers killed thirty men and sunk the whaler Essex in 1820 in the Pacific, no doubt the inspiration for Melville's Pequod.

"Art thou the man to pitch a harpoon down a live whale's throat and then jump after it? Answer quick!" demands one of Melville's characters of a young recruit. But not all whales struck fear among early whalers. Australian whalers used orcas like falcons. The orca slapped its tail when a humpback was near. The whalers killed it and towed it back to shore, allowing the orca to eat the tongue. Legend says the orca even towed the whalers out to sea to help them get the kill.

The one thing about whales that Man always seems to have known, however, was that large prey meant large profits, which is why whaling continues today. An account from 1690 England reported that businessmen observing whales said simply that "there is green pasture where our children's grand-children will go for bread." Melville reported the value to the economy of whaling in the 1850s in America—"shares being held by old annuitants; widows, fatherless children, and chancery wards; each owning a timber, a plank, a nail or two of the ship investing the same way you do now in approved state stocks bringing in good interest." Indeed, "almost all the tapers, lamps, and candles that burn round the globe burn as so many shrines…to the glory of whalers," Melville wrote.

Even as modern commerce is addicted to petroleum and sacrifices more of its wealth and principles every day to secure new supplies of it, it was the oil contained in whales that made them so valuable to our ancestors. Long before the discovery of petroleum, the global economy was powered by whale oil. Ahab's obsession was no different than the CEO of a major oil company today—and the getting of the prize took as much greed and the resulting willingness to convert the resource to cash as fast as possible with no regard for the future.

A scrappy second-string sea captain by the name of Charles Scammon stumbled on the gray whale calving lagoon in Baja Mexico that now bears his name and created a highly profitable whaling assembly line that rivaled anything Henry Ford would later create for the profitable mass production of cars. Just before the Civil War, that once-secret and safe lagoon was home to some 20,000 gray whales. By February 1871, when Scammon wrote in the Overland Monthly that he thought the slaughter of so many whales resulted in their learning to swim farther offshore, he made the fateful observation and query… "their mammoth bones lie bleaching on the shores of those silvery waters and are scattered along the broken coasts from Siberia to the Gulf of California, and ere long, may it not be that the California gray will be known only as one of the extinct species of the Pacific cetaceans?"

If that passed for remorse, Scammon showed none in two whaling seasons from 1859 to 1860, when he slaughtered so many grays that he took 8,200 barrels of oil worth $123,000—equal to $400 million today—and virtually wiped out the grays in the lagoon. He was not alone in hunting living barrels of oil along the California coast. So valuable was whale oil to the economy at the time, it was a whale rush, not the gold rush, that propelled San Francisco to global, glittery prominence.

San Francisco quickly became a major whaling center, situated perfectly in the midst of hundreds of miles of shore stations where whaling was conducted with relative ease, taking mostly cows and calves. From 1855-1865 so many were taken that the industry rapidly declined and died altogether, because of shortages of whales, by the mid 1870s. When steam machines arrived in 1919 another effort was made and six hundred more whales were taken in two seasons, destroying the very source of the enterprise once again.

When the oil was taken, the meat was discarded, with one contemporary account recording that so many butchered remains littered the beaches "fattening clouds of buzzards and vultures." Whalebone was so common along the coast that the courtyard of the San Carlos Mission in Carmel is paved with them.

As grays were hunted to near extinction, San Francisco's Arctic Oil Works turned to refining oil from other whales and elephant seals to continue the production of lighting fuels and lubricants. The business was thought capable of "boundless extension," so great was the faith in what appeared to be the inexhaustible resources of the sea. An artist's rendering of the refinery looks very similar to today's petroleum refineries, complete with belching clouds of black smoke. Baleen was dried on the docks for corset stays, collars, umbrellas, and ironically, buggy whips. As industry converted from horses to engines and from whale oil to petroleum, it also converted from buggy whips to the gas pedal. An 1861 cartoon in Vanity Fair foreshadowed this massive industrial transformation, depicting whales dressed as high-society tycoons toasting the discovery of petroleum with bubbly glasses of champagne.

Even though whaling for oil faded into history, by 1986 only ten percent of the populations of commercially important whale species, including grays, were still alive. As a result, the International Whaling Commission banned commercial whaling that year. Since then, over twenty-five thousand more whales were killed by non-participating nations, such as Norway and Iceland, or under the guise of scientific research by countries such as Japan. With the return of native whaling in several countries, the threat to whales from human hunters is not a thing of history books and hair-raising old novels.

With Peter's arrival at the mouth of Ballona Creek, JJ seemed even more alert and energetic. There was no fog and the sun warmed both our spirits and wetsuit-clad bodies. January weather in southern California, one day like London and the next like Miami. JJ also seemed warmed and joyful, resuming her practice of swimming from one boat to the other, looking for a nipple, but also simply engaging us with eye contact in what might have been some primitive attempt to get us to come out and play. If it was, she succeeded—Peter abruptly shut down his motor and jumped into the water.

JJ made no attempt to swim away as Peter ran his hands over her body, the two of them swimming in an interspecies pas de deux. Although nearly six feet tall, Peter looked tiny compared to the great gray body in the water beside him. The two splashed and swam in circles, Peter laughing with a boyish joy that belied his serious effort to evaluate her condition. The mood changed when our two marine radios crackled to life as one.

"Swimmer in the water with the whale, you are violating the Marine Mammal Protection Act," the static-covered male voice blurted out sternly. "Leave the water immediately."

Of the many onlookers on the beach, one was Terry Rogaczewski, a 27-year-old part time staffer for NMFS, who was now apparently in contact with Joe Cordaro. Rogaczewski had been fumbling around the beach episodically for the past twenty-four hours, but now felt empowered to exert his tenuous authority, even if it contributed nothing to the rescue.

"Get us permission to rescue this whale," I barked over my radio at Rogaczewski, as Peter scrambled back onto his boat. "SeaWorld is ready to take her and I think it's time the media knew who was holding this rescue up."

"Stand by, BayKeeper," Rogaczewski replied sheepishly.

In the hope that we would get the chance to take her to SeaWorld, I had radioed Kris to get a volunteer with a truck capable of lifting a whale and transporting it safely a hundred twenty miles down the freeway to San Diego. Not surprisingly, none of our regulars owned any such heavy equipment—but that did not deter the least likely among them.

Rima Heifetz-Loewe was petite, forty-something, and athletic, yet softened around the edges by a love of painting and sculpture. She cared for animals of all kinds, volunteering at the Santa Barbara Zoo and local animal rescue groups, where she learned a fearlessness and dedication that would pay off with this new challenge of finding a truck for a whale. After getting her hands very dirty with giraffes, red pandas, sea lions, big birds, and the occasional dolphin—how hard could a whale be? she thought. In short, Rima was perfect for the assignment.

After numerous derisive laughs and a few indignant hang-ups, Rima scored a twenty foot panel van with a hoist capable of lifting a ton—just enough for baby JJ. She rented the truck with her own credit card, one of the few in our circle that had one, and dutifully brought it to the road that dead-ends at the beach, about hundred yards from the water's edge. It was shortly before noon, the sun had turned both the beach and the air unusually warm for mid-January, when she gave us the news that the truck was ready. Two minutes later, the radio crackled with another message.

"BayKeeper, this is Terry Rogaczewski, on-scene coordinator," the disembodied voice uttered haltingly. Rogaczewski had given himself a promotion. "Uh, come in please?"

"BayKeeper here."

"Terry, this is Terry. Oh, I think you already know that...I said that...well, good news. Joe just gave permission to try and get the whale on the truck for SeaWorld."

"Thanks, Terry," I replied, truly elated. "Can Rima drive the truck to the water's edge?"

"Well, no. The tires will get stuck in the sand, especially with the weight of the whale on it. But the guy from the Natural History Museum is still here with his flatbed that has four-wheel drive."

That was the answer. Rogaczewski convinced John Heyning to drive his flatbed truck to the shoreline. We would get JJ on that truck first, then get her across the sand to the larger enclosed truck. This might just work, but only if we had a lot of extra hands to carefully wrangle whale, surf, two boats, and two trucks.

"You better come down here," I radioed Kris at HQ. "And bring as much help as you can muster." In less than half an hour, she appeared on the beach waving to us, standing alongside Beverly and a ragtag group of BayKeeper volunteers, who were normally asked to do nothing more dramatic for us than grab a small sample of stormwater for pollution analysis. Gathering around them like a parade on St. Patrick's Day were lifeguards, skaters, surfers, tourists, cops, homeless guys, fishermen, and beachfront condo owners. Most were unsure what was being asked of them, but all eyes were gazing towards two boats and a whale.

With Peter's boat on one side and mine on the other, JJ had been swimming slowly in whatever direction we moved, much as she had done for the past thirty-six hours of her young life. Trusting her only living companions, she seemed completely unconcerned as we moved carefully into shallow water, then shallower still, aiming for the two hundred hands now waiting on the beach. The flatbed truck was ready; a sling cobbled together from several stretchers used for human rescues; cables to the winch on the truck to pull the contraption if we ever got her into it.

When the boats were mere feet from grounding, JJ rolled over on one side and looked up. Whatever she understood, there was no struggle, only peaceful surrender as she stayed perfectly positioned between the two boats. By contrast, the beach was a sea of commotion and hectic activity. Peter and I jumped into the water and waded the final few yards with our baby gray whale. In a minute, we were all in the mercifully gentle surf, half afloat, half beached. People gasped, yelled, cried, cheered. Cameras rolled and snapped. Peter shouted commands.

Figure 12: *JJ comes ashore (Wallerstein in foreground; auther in back)*

Figure 13a: *JJ in the sling*

Patiently, gently, the lifeguards and strongest of the volunteers helped us slide the stretcher beneath her, careful to avoid scraping her tender skin as much as we could. No one had ever seen people with so many different stripes come together and do something as one, coordinated, ego-less organism. Out of our depth, literally and figuratively, we all fell silent and started listening both to Peter and the needs of a helpless creature.

"Terry get the tail," Peter barked. All hands were at her head and body as we lifted the makeshift stretcher, but the tail folded under flaccidly and Peter feared she might be injured. Kris and I rushed to support her tail, joined instantly by an old woman in a bright blue windbreaker, as the procession moved slowly to the edge of the truck bed, which was now tilted at a forty-five degree angle. It was like a military operation, except nothing had been planned or rehearsed. Peter just

Figure 13b: *Author with JJ onshore*

figured out what needed to be done, as he had improvised with marine mammal rescues for a decade, and calmly led us through it.

John Heyning was waiting with the winch cable, which he quickly connected to the ends of the stretcher. The motor came to life, grinding and smoking under the weight, but somehow managed to drag the suspended whale onto the platform of the truck, taking her weight as we relinquished it, two hands, then ten, then fifty, until she was laying completely on the flatbed. Heyning raced to the cab and engaged the controls to level the bed. In a minute, JJ was horizontal in the back of the truck, flanked by a dozen human bodies, which kept her from rolling off as Beverly thoughtfully splashed water on her exposed back and sides.

Figure 13c: *Hoisting JJ onto Heyning's flatbed*

Peter and I had to get our boats out of the surf to keep them from swamping, so JJ's fate was now in the hands of others. There was no time for goodbyes or sentiment as the tall, fat, old, athletic, men, girls, Hispanic, Anglo, black, Asian, you-name-it volunteers took over seamlessly, as if they had done it together a thousand times before.

Rima waited nervously at the rented truck, having left her shiny Lexus in a not-so-nice neighborhood for what she thought would be

Figure 13d: *JJ on the flatbed truck*

an hour or two at most. Nervous because she had never driven a truck before, and because she barely got this one from the rental yard to the beach without collision, the sweat of her palms still glistening on the steering wheel. She assumed one of us would take over for her, but as the person whose name was on the contract and whose American Express card was at risk, she was actually the only one authorized to drive it. There was no time to wait for me or Peter to dock our boats and join her. She slowly realized the task belonged to her alone.

Her fretting was quickly dispelled by the arrival of Heyning's flatbed, backing up to the rear of her rental truck. Volunteers ran alongside like a detail of Secret Service, others were on the truck with JJ. Hundreds of onlookers followed, kicking up sand, tumbling, shouting, snapping pictures. Kids hopped up and down, trying to get a glimpse of JJ, who lay quietly on her bier, the center of the Macy's Thanksgiving Day parade, a real life balloon, no helium-filled fantasy.

Once again, two hundred hands grasped every part of whale and sling and shuffled her from one truck to the next. Kris and Rima had cobbled together a bed of wet foam and blankets, conscripted door-to-door from houses and apartments along the strand, then had the

Figure 13e: *Two hundred hands and more*

presence of mind to fill buckets with seawater and load them in with
JJ. Two volunteers hunkered down with the soggy cargo, determined
to keep her calm and her skin moist. One was a US Attorney who had
been on a bike ride down the beach when he came upon the unusual
scene, the other a New York man who had brought his father's ashes
to be cast upon the waters of the Pacific. The roll door of the truck
slammed down and two policemen hoisted Rima back into the cab.
California Highway Patrol motorcycles already had their flashing lights
on and roared their engines. The caravan crept away from the beach,
Kris and Beverly at the center of a giant farewell committee waving,
crying, and cheering, and gathered speed toward the freeway.

JJ's breathing was labored at times, so shallow at other times as to
be imperceptible. Her inexperienced caretakers were never sure if she
was alive, dead, or slowly shifting between the two. Her skin seemed
to drape over her rib cage and her eyes, although closed most of the
time, bulged from her skull. She remained eerily calm, as if she knew
something the rest of us could not about her fate.

Two Los Angeles police patrol cars took over the escort duty as
the truck climbed the onramp of the San Diego freeway. Police and

news helicopters overhead kept cameras trained on the procession, the whack-whack-whack of blades always audible to Rima and the occupants of her truck. At the Orange County line, local officers took over the duty, seamlessly passing the responsibility from one to the other, clearing traffic and maintaining a steady seventy miles per hour.

Rima had been operating on adrenaline, but as the driving became uneventful and hypnotic, she began to feel shaken, tired and cold. She remembered the OJ Simpson slow-speed freeway chase, wondering what other drivers thought was in a rented truck that was so important, or dangerous, as to deserve a similar police escort in front, behind, and above. The bright afternoon gave way to a dim January evening and fog rolled sporadically across the road as the caravan moved into San Diego County and new police cars took control.

After nearly two hours, the freeway exit sign read "SeaWorld." Rima focused on the taillights of the police car in front of her, fearful that she would take a wrong turn in the dark and end up where she couldn't maneuver. She sat up ramrod straight with a grip so tight on the wheel that her hands had turned white. As they passed through the gates of SeaWorld, the dark winter sky suddenly glowed with camera lights and a thousand well-wishers, fighting off the dank cold with rays of hope that JJ had survived the trip.

With guidance from a traffic cop waving two red flashlights, Rima managed to back the truck up to the loading dock, where SeaWorld staff and veterinarians waited with a sling designed for large whales and a crane to match. Rima shut off the engine as the door of her truck was quickly rolled open. Falling out of the cab, she heard the words she had prayed would come at the end of this ordeal.

"She's alive," someone yelled from the back. "The whale is alive!" Rima slumped to the running board and wept. A Highway Patrolman came over to thank and reassure her.

"You did it, little lady," the burly officer pronounced, a hand on her shoulder as he bent forward to meet her gaze. "You did some fine driving there and you should know how rare what you did actually is—we have never done a full escort like that down a state highway for anyone less than the President or the Pope. Now you and your whale are in some high-falutin' company."

Rima took a hot cup of coffee from someone and mumbled a few words of thanks to the officer. She had wanted so desperately to make this rescue work. The hundreds of birds and other animals she had helped were important, but she never felt such kinship with another species in her life. The pitiful sight of JJ rolling in the surf a few hours earlier, lost and simply wanting its mother, hungry and exhausted. It was really just a baby—and the mother in Rima had decided that she would have to be the one to care for it.

As the SeaWorld staff took over, the ragged rescue transformed to practiced precision. Half a dozen wet-suited staff stood in waist deep water as the crane gracefully transferred the whale from truck to pool, flukes poking through openings in the specially designed canvas sling. She may not survive her ordeal, but she was in the best of human hands imaginable at this moment.

As volunteers and the curious in San Diego and Marina del Rey dispersed, returning to their own struggles to survive, JJ's rescue lingered as a question mark. Why do whales matter more to us than other living things? Why save this one?

Yes, whales may serve as a canary in the mineshaft, a species that foretells the fate of humanity on the ocean planet we share, and therefore reason enough to save one, to save one thousand. But our emotions about saving JJ that day may betray another very human quality—a sense of fairness. Until modern science gave us the means to measure our impact on the natural world, we could be forgiven for destroying so much of it for our own profit or pleasure. But today no such excuse exists, we know better, and whether our hand is in an off-limits cookie jar or we are faced with allowing one more whale to die, the human sense of fair play kicks in and surpasses other needs and wants, at least for a day.

In the fourth Star Trek movie, the crew of the Enterprise goes back in time to capture a whale and bring it to their twenty-fourth century to answer a call from an alien probe. Humans are not the only intelligent life form in Earth's history, indeed thoughtless humans in the twenty-first century wiped out humpback whales, according to the story, implying that the humans were far less evolved than the creatures they exterminated. JJ's future was not science fiction however. Only the best of science fact—and a large amount of luck—could write a happy ending to this unusual melodrama.

Chapter 6

FOOTPRINTS ON WATER

When whales dive, they leave a distinctive footprint on the surface that lingers for several minutes, a massive upwelling of water that continues longer the deeper they dive. Blue whales, the largest living creatures ever to leave any kind of footprint on earth, leave broad shoals of still water like calm islands in any kind of sea, no matter how wind-swept or choppy. JJ left footprints commensurate with her size and shallow dives when we watched her in the waters near the marina, dissolving into the swell and wavelets of the Bay as if they were merely an illusion.

Her survival now seemed as ephemeral as those footprints. She arrived at SeaWorld that cool January afternoon, lifted from the rented truck like a sack of flour with nary a wiggle or protest. Some onlookers thought her already dead. She was comatose, perhaps a blessing, and remained placid and compliant. As she was floated in a tank of water, caressed by her new human companions, she seemed weak and unable to move on her own, her skin now no more than a cadaverous gray-white and infested with lice.

Her new caretakers, clad in wetsuits with SeaWorld logos depicting obedient orcas leaping over swelling waves, steered her body around the forty by forty foot tank, virtual swimming in no more than four feet of water to keep her blowhole above water to prevent drowning. Blood was drawn and the vets examined the cuts and ulcers on several parts of her body, quickly surmising the obvious—she was severely dehydrated and malnourished. The good news was that tests showed no infection or disease that might sap more of her meager strength.

Within half an hour, she opened her eyes and started swimming slowly on her own. Most theme park marine mammals die within two years of capture for a variety of reasons, but for all of them, the first few days in confinement determine their future prospects. JJ was officially weighed and measured during her transfer to the tank—a "scrawny" 1671 pounds and fourteen feet in length. SeaWorld's experts predicted that JJ would not survive the night.

"The prognosis for a full recovery is no better than poor," SeaWorld spokesman Dr. Jim McBain told reporters soon after her arrival.

McBain and his team would try everything to beat the odds. They began by feeding her gruel every two hours through a tube thrust into her mouth, two gallons of a foul-smelling milk shake, a pastiche of fat-rich ground herring, heads removed, heavy whipping cream, sugar, salt, antibiotics, and vitamins. Much of the mixture gurgled out of her mouth, just as it had for Gigi many years earlier at SeaWorld, so as JJ became more responsive, the tube was snaked down her throat and directly into her stomach to ensure that nutrients would quickly be absorbed.

With each passing hour, JJ grew noticeably stronger and more responsive. She chomped at the rubber tube and pressed her massive tongue against hose, hands, and formula in greedy attempts to consume more and more. Even as her prognosis brightened, that of another fragile creature was fading.

Judy Jones was a registered nurse who managed Friends of the Sea Lion and had participated in countless marine mammal rescues of her own. On JJ's second day at SeaWorld, Judy died unexpectedly at the age of fifty-one. Two days later, JJ had made enough progress to justify her new caretakers giving her a name—she was named after the selfless friend of many ocean creatures. As the announcement was made and the newly christened "JJ" completed her first week at SeaWorld, over eleven thousand calls were logged to ask about her progress.

Even a week's survival was a small miracle, given how little we actually know about gray whales in general and newborns in particular. The story was brought into sharper focus when another baby gray whale was seen only a mile away, entangled in nets off the coast of San Diego, just a week after JJ arrived at SeaWorld. While waiting for permission from NMFS to rescue the infant, it died and sank to the bottom of the sea, never to be seen again.

Such stark contrasts and the singular connection felt by those who came into physical contact with JJ stirred strong emotions in her human allies. But what was JJ feeling and sensing? She had experienced so little of her mother, of other whales, of any kind of natural surroundings. Did the shallow tank and lethargic maneuvering among neoprene-clad humans seem normal? In the wild, she would be surrounded in three dimensions with an infinite assortment of smells of birth/death, sounds received and returned, fast-moving fish and diving birds, sea lions barking, waves crashing and swells lifting/falling, and endless room to swim. As an orphan though, she would not have survived in that world. Instead, with a slim hope to live, she was confined to a sterile tank of silence and little more than enough breadth and depth to turn a full circle.

As a rainy January became a cool, dull February, JJ completed three weeks in this environment and weighed 1840 pounds, still several hundred pounds lighter than normal. Those of us who felt conflicted about SeaWorld's record of exploiting captured marine mammals were grateful that they had invested so much care and funding to nurture this one lonely infant. SeaWorld had saved her from death, from pollution and a shrinking habitat, even from whaling. Her counterparts across the Pacific would live in fear of becoming school lunch on the plates of Japanese students. Instead, JJ would become a celebrity next door to other marine mammals that perform tricks for treats in front of thousands of adoring fans.

"The rehabilitation of JJ is almost like walking on the moon," Jim Antrim said with his usual hand-up-in-class enthusiasm. "Right after

I started at SeaWorld, they captured Gigi and they learned a bit from that, but this was all new. We jumped right in—I was in Vietnam and learned early in life that you don't wait around for things to happen, you just have to act."

It was JJ's fans and her steady growth—to twenty-five hundred pounds—that prompted Antrim to look for larger quarters for his new charge. He knew that marine mammal protection law forbid SeaWorld from public display or profit using rehabilitating animals like JJ, but Antrim also saw that he had both a PR bonanza and a practical space problem on his hands. The only place large enough to hold JJ for several more months of care and feeding was a large public stadium pool called "Shamu Backstage." There was no practical way to exclude the public from this part of the park, nor would his corporate bosses take kindly to putting a costly facility off-limits to paying customers for a summer for private nursing. The Vietnam vet once again took action.

"I called Cordaro at NMFS and told him that JJ was growing so quickly that, like a snake, her skin kept cracking and peeling off," he said dramatically. "I made it clear she would only survive if we could move her to the larger pool and he finally agreed."

A month after her arrival at SeaWorld, JJ was carefully coaxed back into the sling and craned acrobatically into the Shamu Backstage theatre pool, a larger tank—1.7 million gallons and thirty-two feet deep—that resembled an ice hockey rink, outfitted with a large underwater viewing window to facilitate her human well-wishers that now flooded the turnstiles. What did a baby whale think of cheering crowds, music, and the smell of popcorn and hot dogs? As she lifted her head above the water, what did she make of the encircling grey concrete, fake rocks, grandstands, a few small trees and a small grass hut where the trainers stood to perform? Was she intimidated by the sound of orcas in the even larger stadium-style tank next door, which was connected by a deep channel and separated only by a metal trap door?

"Well, at first JJ showed a little reluctance to explore the large Shamu Backstage," Antrim said to a webcam on the SeaWorld website that had been set up so that even the most remote visitor could marvel at their prize—thousands of viewers hit the website in the first few days, even in 1997 when few had the high-speed web access we enjoy today. "Then, slowly but surely after a few hours, she seemed quite comfortable going to all areas of the backstage pool."

Behind Antrim on the video is the glass wall revealing the underwater expanse of the pool, crowded with visitors leaning on the glass, a mosh pit of rapidly moving arms, heads, legs, sticky hands, steamy breath, rising squeals, elbows/knees/palms banged on glass, and all things mystifying to any creature on the watery side of the divide.

Peter Wallerstein called SeaWorld several times to ask about JJ's progress, each time hoping someone would acknowledge his role in her rescue and invite him to visit. At the same time, he was angry that he felt beholden to this theme park that he had spent so many years fighting. His campaigns sought to expose the harshness of life for captive marine mammals, but now JJ's survival depended on their skill and largesse. In the end, he decided not to visit, with or without an invitation.

But the general public did visit, watching and recording JJ's every move with no such emotional conflict. By March, she was gaining over a pound an hour and the vets made her formula thicker to begin the transition to solid food. After two months in captivity, she weighed over thirty-two hundred pounds and measured nearly seventeen feet long, a gain of fifteen hundred pounds and three feet since coming to SeaWorld. She rolled to one side when she suckled the plastic tube that delivered her food, one flipper out of the water looking at the humans with curiosity. She began to scrape against the wall of the tank, reminiscent of the moves she made on our patrol boats in the marina, still looking for a mother's nipple.

The vets feared she would injure herself, so they made a plastic water-filled bladder and hung it from the side of the tank, feeding her from there to simulate whale-to-whale contact as she suckled from the milk hose. Her handlers were pleased with the arrangement, because they wanted to prevent JJ from associating humans with food on the assumption she would one day be returned to the wild. She often nudged the plastic "mother whale" so lovingly it burst and had to be replaced.

With her health apparently stable, SeaWorld tried to learn what they could from this orphan that had washed up on their doorstop. With Gigi several years earlier, SeaWorld hired college basketball players with long arms to investigate whale anatomy, palpating the lungs and heart by thrusting their hands through her mouth and rectum, not an unusual technique with large animals, but it must have been very uncomfortable nonetheless. With JJ, the park staff began with less invasive tests.

Ann Bowles, of the Hubbs-SeaWorld Research Institute, started playing gray whale sounds to her, but had no idea if it was gibberish. She also listened patiently to JJ's sounds and discovered something astonishing for a whale that had little or no contact with other whales—her "speech" sounded a lot like adult gray whales, including the unique popping sounds that are thought to aid in navigation. Gigi had also made sounds that were not normal for a juvenile, but she had spent many months with her own kind.

Whales "speak" in many "languages"—humpbacks sound like violins and orcas like operatic sopranos, pitched eight times higher than any human diva. Only grays speak in the same range as humans. Individual gray groans and squeaks last only a tenth of a second, grouped into about five beats at a time, the resulting sound richly textured with vibrato. In other sounds, that could come from just about any human, they also whistle and grunt. They gurgle like percolating coffee and early whalers heard hammering sounds, as if on a wooden hull, wondering if the whales had learned it from carpenters plying their trade on the whaling ships. It may have been so, for in modern times, grays have been heard issuing distinctive bubbling sounds that mimic outboard motors. Was JJ's speech an attempt to mimic and communicate with us?

Perhaps the most striking similarity with human speech, however, is that grays talk continuously—in one study they were recorded communicating with each other for thirteen uninterrupted days and nights. Unlike humans, gray whales use sound to move, increasing chatter to each other when they encounter obstacles and echo-locating with clicks like a thumbnail running along the teeth of a comb. Gigi made these clicking noises upon her return to the wild—sounds she had never made in the tank at SeaWorld. It was as if she didn't speak "whale" in the tank, knowing there were no others of her kind nearby, but the moment she was released she began calling to locate her family and acquaintances. We'll never know what, if any, replies she received.

In some ways, grays communicate neither like humans nor other whales, but with subtle tones unlike any other species in the world. Mothers have distinctive calls to their calves, soft/tender tones that resemble a distant Chinese gong, sounds that are made only in protected birthing lagoons, perhaps teaching their young an "indoor voice."

JJ made an impressive array of all of these, despite having so little exposure to any living being of her kind. She also made a sound that Bowles recognized immediately from recordings in calving lagoons when grays were agitated—JJ protested the same "annoyance" signal when SeaWorld veterinarians drew blood. At least at those times, she was definitely trying to communicate with the humans.

"JJ gave us the keys to what was instinctive in gray whale newborns and what was learned," said Vicki Floyd, marine biologist and whale sound expert. "From the time the calf was three months old, we'd play for her other gray whale vocalizations recorded in the birthing lagoons and the Chukchi and Bering Seas. Then we'd reinforce those vocalizations with food so she would associate gray whale sounds with feeding. Upon release, we hope she will follow gray whales and find her own food."

The humans who studied JJ with such curiosity were indeed beginning to think about sending her back to her own kind, but the ones who studied the public response to the orphan—and the profits at the park that began to swell—were thinking of another option. By mid-April, at three months of age, JJ shot past eighteen feet long and forty-two hundred pounds, but SeaWorld executives began to wonder out loud if it was possible to keep her for many more months, or even years, to come.

SeaWorld asked a variety of experts and even held a conference to debate the matter in full view of JJ at her underwater theatre. As spring gave way to summer and the tens of thousands of eager tourists, the financial bonanza was too great to ignore. Still, one by one the experts advised SeaWorld to plan for her release. By June, SeaWorld management agreed to milk what they could for a summer, but to let her go in the fall. It may have been SeaWorld's experience with Gigi that reminded management how big these creatures can get.

They had learned other things from Gigi that were now useful with their rapidly growing superstar. Gigi displayed normal feeding behavior without a teacher, scooping food from the bottom of her tank without prompting, so it was reasonable to hope that JJ would be likewise hard-wired. Her handlers began leaving piles of capelin, krill, and squid on the bottom of her tank. She continued to suckle, but soon showed a preference for the fresh seafood. Like most grays and humans, JJ was a rightie, preferring to scoop the food with the right side of her massive, six-foot long jaw. Within a few weeks, she completely abandoned the nipple on her water-filled plastic bag "mother."

Figure 14a: *JJ at SeaWorld*

By August, she was eating about five hundred pounds a day of herring, squid, krill, and sardines—some 150,000 calories worth. She quickly grew to twenty-six feet and almost thirteen thousand pounds. At the same age, Gigi—who had been taken violently from her mother and pod in the wild—was several feet shorter and half the weight. JJ had been in captivity for eight months and seemed to also enjoy snacks of shrimp fed to her by the bucket-load by her handlers for photographers and shrieking kids. Within another month, she was eating almost half a ton of food each day.

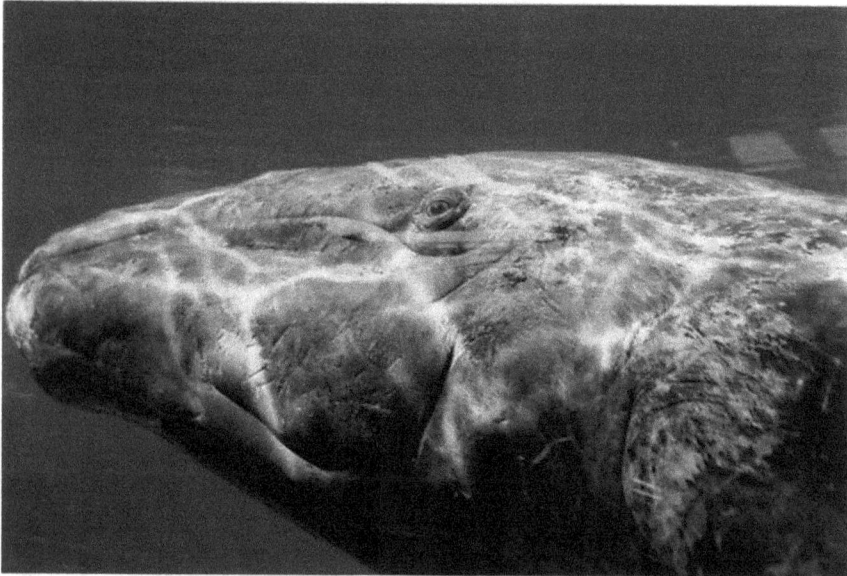

Figure 14b: *Close up of JJ at SeaWorld*

"Thank you for calling SeaWorld San Diego, home of JJ the baby gray whale," spouted the recorded voice on SeaWorld's main phone line. The automaton went on to describe the times, places, and myriad ways that humans could get their fill of the park's star whale attraction. The gift shop was populated with JJ memorabilia that would rival Mickey Mouse at a Disney store. Every corner of the park linked to some aspect of JJ's presence to make visitors feel they had encountered her more than anyone actually did. The line snaked hundreds of feet to get a glimpse of her through the giant viewing window beneath the surface or from the edges of the pool above. JJ cost SeaWorld vast amounts of money for her care and feeding, but she was returning a handsome profit on the investment, both in dollars and public relations.

By December, nearly a year after her rescue, JJ had grown to thirty feet and about nine tons. With the onset of cooler weather the crowds thinned and JJ's handlers could no longer delay serious planning for her release. It was decided to put her back in the ocean in early spring, hoping she would connect with a pod of gray whales migrating northward.

The US military had long been interested in using marine mammals to spy underwater and SeaWorld had been training sea lions to maneuver video cameras in various ocean settings. They decided to use them to follow JJ at her release, so they began introducing them to her in her tank, little by little. At first she showed no concern as the sea lions were tethered to prevent them from getting too close. Over time the whale and the sea lions interacted, touching and swimming freely, cameras whirring and some inter-species communication developing.

But sea lion interlopers with cameras were no substitute for the companionship of other gray whales or the rich texture of the open ocean itself and it had become clear that there was little more that researchers could learn from a captive whale. Indeed the greatest lesson from the entire JJ experiment may have been that we can learn much more by studying her kind in the wild. After a year in captivity, SeaWorld had collected her blood to make antibody serum for future stranded or ailing whales; Russian scientists concluded that whales dream; and when they opened JJ's tank to the adjacent orca pool, she exhibited a visceral fear that must be genetic, because she had no life experience with these predators. Beyond that, whale science didn't advance much from holding JJ captive for most of 1997, but she was alive and healthy enough to go home.

Much was changing about the world since we first encountered JJ a year ago. Ice was discovered on the moon, meaning there was at least one other heavenly body composed in part of water. Whether it was scientifically feasible or not, nineteen European nations passed a law to forbid human cloning. In a specter of things to come, Iraq's President Saddam Hussein allowed UN inspectors to look for weapons of mass destruction in Baghdad, avoiding threatened US military action. Princess Diana had been killed in a car crash in Paris. The first color photograph appeared on the front page of the New York Times. The Kyoto Protocol to address global warming was adopted by nearly 200 nations. The Toyota Prius went on sale in Japan. Some things unsettling, others clearly hopeful, much like JJ's recovery but uncertain future.

On Martin Luther King Jr. Day in mid-January 1998, Jim Antrim received another distress call, much like the one a year earlier that led him to JJ. This time it was an infant gray whale, disoriented and alone in the waters near San Diego's Mission Bay. With no government resources available on a federal holiday, Antrim recruited two SeaWorld divers and piloted a small boat out to the animal's reported location. His efforts to radio Joe Cordaro, or anyone at NMFS for guidance, were unsuccessful and he could do no more than observe when he found the young whale.

Antrim learned that the Mission Bay lifeguards had a buoy tender that was large enough to hoist the whale onto its deck for a possible transfer to SeaWorld—perhaps giving his theme park a replacement for JJ, who would be gone in a few weeks—but the twenty-four hour rule prevented anyone from attempting to capture it. By the next morning, when officials were back in their cubicles and the whale had not repatriated with its own kind, the drama ended as suddenly as it began. Stressed and emaciated from an unknown period of struggling to survive solo, the young whale simply couldn't wait any longer. It had perished overnight.

In February 1998, thirteen months after her birth and rescue, JJ had grown to thirty-one feet and over ten tons—the largest marine mammal ever held in captivity. If her human handlers needed any more evidence that she had grown too large for her virtual ocean, they got it by her own behavior. As the winter wore on, JJ had become noticeably listless and she was often seen floating on one side. Veterinarians tested and prodded, trainers offered distractions and fish treats, but nothing changed her demeanor. Was she depressed? Was there a medical reason? At last, one of the trainers realized that every time she floated aimlessly in the tank it was actually anything but aimless. She was always pointing north. Previous research had discovered iron oxides in gray whale brains—tiny magnetic particles—a compass. JJ was pointing north at the very time her kin were doing likewise.

With little left to accomplish for her, with less left to learn from her captivity, JJ was physically and emotionally ready to leave SeaWorld. Her once sleek pale gray skin was now mottled shades of black and white. Her rubbery body now reflected the contours of maturity— soccer ball patterned dimples for a "nose"; long furrowed wrinkles stretching many feet from her chin to beneath her flippers; knuckled ridges where other whales had dorsal fins; randomly spaced scars from scratching herself against cement walls; a sparse array of short wiry white hairs on the top of her head; a full mouth of white lace-like baleen for straining food onto a massive pink tongue; a snowy white "soul patch" of white growths where humans sport moustaches and goatees on her upper jaw and chin. Her massive tail and flukes looked like they might propel a battleship. With her mouth closed, she appeared to grin like a kid with one hand in the cookie jar. Her bulging black round eyes, expressively encased beneath humanoid eyelids and a forward slanting brow, gave every human who saw her the sense that she was looking only at them.

None of us could know her thoughts. But all of us knew it was time to say goodbye and trust her to the ocean, despite the indignities and indifference that humankind thrusts upon it. As target dates for her release were debated, a decision was made thousands of miles away that might end her life in the wild before it could really begin.

Men with spears had almost exterminated gray whales from the eastern Pacific a hundred years before. If JJ was now returned to the wild, she would need to survive a very similar threat from a very unlikely source.

Chapter 7

CAPTIVE NO MORE?

"If you could write a fable for little fishes," said Melville in Moby Dick, "you would make them speak like great whales." And if great whales might speak, what would they tell us? As the day for her release grew closer, JJ might have spoken a few words of protest when her skin was pierced to attach two radios, like a teenager getting navel and nose rings. Her handlers hoped to track her movements, backed up by the trained sea lions with cameras that were assigned to shadow her first days in the wild.

At fourteen months of age, JJ was no teenager, but at least a normal gray whale-sized youth. SeaWorld had done about all it could for her—restored her health, taught her to feed from the bottom, exposed her to an eclectic collection of other sea life and the voices of her own kind. The staff, veterinarians, and customers had showered her with affection, which may have been felt by her at some level. Did she understand what the humans had done for her or reciprocate their feelings? Or was she just increasingly eager to be free and head north? Her compass-like behavior had continued throughout the early spring and the date for her release was now set for the end of March.

"Some people have suggested it'll be like watching your children go off to school for the first time," said Tom Reidarson, SeaWorld's chief veterinarian wistfully. "It's not. Your children come home again."

Joe Cordaro of NMFS coordinated the release with other federal authorities, including the US Coast Guard that provided a buoy tender to ferry JJ to her release point. He hoped she would connect to a pod of grays heading north and learn whatever whale skills were still missing from her repertoire. More than joining the traveling circus and catching on to the tricks of the trade, JJ would need much more. She would also need luck—because a few hundred miles to the north, the Makah tribe had just been granted the right to harvest a gray whale for the first time in generations.

The Makah have thousand year-old petroglyphs showing whales face-to-face with round, wide-eyed humans. By the mid-1800s, European disease was killing the Makah and European whalers were killing the whales, so that by 1915, tribal elders decided to end whaling, because both the tribe and the herd were so small. A generation later, the International Whaling Commission (IWC) banned commercial whaling completely, but in 1995, the Makah elders petitioned for the right "to fulfill the legacy of our forefathers and restore a part of our culture which was taken from us." Five whales a year, for ceremonial and subsistence purposes, wrote tribal chairman Hubert Markishtum in the petition.

"Maybe some of our young people have become victims of crime and drug or alcohol addiction," he wrote. "A whale hunt wouldn't solve all these problems, and maybe it wouldn't solve any of them, but there are things it could teach. Discipline. Cooperation. Spiritual things. An appreciation for old ways at a time when being Indians is as much a matter of public relations, politics, peer pressure, congressional budgets, fishing rights as it once was harpoons and cedar canons."

The IWC also received a petition from some Makah elders protesting the hunt, asserting that modern tribes no longer needed to take the lives of such kindred beings, especially given that their numbers were still hovering around endangered levels. Other tribes, normally reluctant to intercede in the affairs of neighbors, also felt compelled in this unique case to weigh in too.

"Our tribe fully supports our Makah neighbors in their treaty rights, but our Quileute elders have made a different decision," said

Fred Woodruff of the neighboring Quileute tribe. "Even though we… have the same treaty rights to hunt, our elders have chosen to support the gray whale. For thousands of years, this whale has been valuable under subsistence, but now the value is in its life. The gray whale is more valuable to the Quileutes living than hunted."

After a lengthy battle, both publicly and privately, the Makah were granted the right to take five gray whales each year for five years, starting in the spring of 1998—the time set for JJ's release.

"I want the sea back," said one tribal member, whose Makah name, Stecowilth, means gray whale. "This is my country."

If she made it as far north as the US/Canada border, where the Makah would be re-creating their ancient hunting heritage, JJ would face razor-tipped metal harpoons and guns instead of the helpful humans she had encountered so far. Would she be so naïve as to nudge a Makah boat and roll over to share a glimpse with its occupants, as she had done a year earlier in Marina del Rey with Peter and me? This time, that could cost her life.

Nootka, Makah, Quillayute, Koryak, Inuit, Quinault—all of the tribes of the Pacific northwest—had a rich history of whaling from dugout or skin-covered canoes, or trapping them with nets of walrus skin set at the mouths of inlets. Kodiak Islanders used poisoned-tipped lances and elaborate ceremony to "call" the whales. No living Makah had actually hunted whales, but elders told the new generation of would-be hunters what their parents and grandparents had told them.

The young, eager Makah would revive what had sustained their people for generations, following their tribe's cultural practice. They would be taught that although the spring is the best time to kill the slow-moving whales as they head north, the preparations must begin months earlier. The ceremonial and spiritual aspects were even more important than the physical ones, the elders said, because the Makah would ask the whale to give its life.

The whalers would bathe in cold water all winter, diving beneath the waves and holding their breath as long as they could to feel what it was to be a whale. They toughened their skin by rubbing it with rough hemlock; they fasted, prayed, and abstained from sex. The leader of the whaling clan would pray for a vision, a dream of a whale that would offer itself and say "it is time."

A crew of seven in a cedar canoe would paddle miles offshore, ready with sharp shell-tipped harpoons twice the length of a man. They would pray, listen, and wait. When the whale appeared and the canoe drew close enough, the harpooner would stand on the bow and thrust. His mates would uncoil rope attached to the harpoon and several seal-skin floats. The whale would tow them until it tired and drowned, but not before a member of the clan could swim alongside and sew the animal's lips closed to prevent it taking on water and sinking. When the whalers returned, the entire village would welcome them—and the whale—with song and ceremony, gratefully placing eagle down in the whale's blowhole as an offering of thanks.

With luck, the Makah would not take JJ, nor a pregnant female trying to bring another calf into the world later in the year when the migration again turns southward. The "scientific" whaling allowed in Japan has essentially doubled the deaths that are allowed by law, because seventy percent of the whales taken under that guise are pregnant. Regardless of the many challenges JJ would face in the open sea, the added threat of being hunted was not enough to delay her release. The time had come.

San Diego is blessed with almost year-round perfect weather and March 31, 1998, was no exception. Light jacket weather under bright skies and calm seas. JJ would go home on this postcard day. The absurdly named Conifer, a one-hundred-twenty-foot Coast Guard buoy tender that was accustomed to craning mammoth heavy structures into the air and lowering them into the water, was provided for the task of getting JJ to the open water near Point Loma at the mouth of San Diego Bay. Another large Coast Guard vessel, the Tybee, served as a platform for officials and news media. Seven smaller Coast Guard boats and a helicopter performed security detail and searched for a pod of grays that might be the focus of JJ's release. The US Navy provided a whale-sized dock for the handoff from SeaWorld's truck to the Conifer. Airport authorities restricted air traffic over the scene. The

California Highway Patrol and San Diego police reprised their service of a year ago, serving as traffic escorts and security detail. There wasn't much more humanly possible to make the release a success. The rest was up to JJ.

With the sun barely over the horizon, SeaWorld staff enticed JJ into the sling that she had occupied several times in her young life, either for moves to larger tanks or for medical exams. This time she was lifted onto the bed of a truck that normally carries forty foot long shipping containers, twenty tons of cargo bound for Walmarts or factories many miles inland. Just such a container was stripped of its top and fitted with cushions, like a giant topless coffin, into which JJ was lowered with great care. Her bulk consumed almost all of the available space, laid out with her head facing the path of travel. Every step of the carefully planned choreography was executed in slow motion to make certain that the precious cargo would remain undamaged. Hours passed, the air grew heavier, both literally and figuratively.

Kept cool and wet with a constant spray of water from truck to dock, from crane to the Conifer, and quickly out to sea, JJ made no outward sign of alarm or protest. No grays had been seen in the immediate area, so the captain let his vessel drift to a stop several miles west of San Diego at mid-morning. By now, JJ was visibly agitated, whacking her great tail up and down, flicking her head from side to side within the confines of the sling, as if trying to squirm free. SeaWorld staff and the ship's captain concurred that this was the place and now was the time.

JJ was lifted off the deck and the crane arm rotated to hover a few feet above the waves. With a loud metallic snap, one side of the sling disconnected and her shiny dark body rolled in slow motion away from all things man-made. Some fourteen months after her birth and amazing rescue, JJ was returned to the sea.

To JJ, the sensory inputs from the open ocean must have been as shockingly different as being dropped in the middle of Times Square after spending a life in the solitary confinement cell of a prison. She dove immediately to take it all in and to escape both jail and jailers. For a quarter of an hour, no one aboard the many vessels could see her. The tracking devices worked as expected however, so iridescent screens in the wheelhouse told scientists her whereabouts with digital precision. The captain of the Conifer made a perfunctory announcement that JJ was apparently OK and engaged his engines. The flotilla slowly headed back to harbor.

"JJ did what a wild animal will do," said SeaWorld chief veterinarian Tom Reidarson. "She got the heck away from human beings as fast as she could. It's not that she doesn't like us. It's just that she doesn't need us anymore."

She may not need us to feed and fawn over her, but given the ocean we sent her back to, she will most certainly need human help to survive in the long run. In the Pacific Northwest, along the path of JJ's migration, so many toxins from flame-retardants, pesticides, and coolants are in the sediments that the bodies of countless sea creatures are now contaminated with our waste. As large creatures eat smaller ones, the pollution magnifies until those same toxins make their way into our bodies when we eat seafood. Our bodies contain mercury, PBDs, PCBs, and a host of other alphabet-soup toxins that entered our bodies after first being in the sea. We once thought we could throw things "away"—in a dump or the ocean—but now we know that there is no "away."

Though we can change our diets and try to limit exposure, JJ has no such option. The result is that year after year, these toxins build up to higher and higher levels in whales, despite the fact that human destruction of the food sources themselves has resulted in less nutrition overall and whales that are visibly thinner in many places of the world. In essence, because of human activities, the ocean is running out of the ability to sustain something so large as a whale, much as the earth once lost its capacity to sustain dinosaurs.

"If the oceans a few hundred years ago could support a hundred thousand gray whales, why can't the oceans sustain twenty thousand whales today?" said Stephen Palumbi, a Stanford University professor who figured out that gray whale populations are nowhere near historic levels, despite some respite from whaling. He found similar results for humpback, fin and minke whales in the North Atlantic—they once numbered at least ten times more than today's populations.

The answers are an intricate web of sequential cause and effect. Off the coast of Africa alone, for example, factory trawlers gobble up a hundred billion sardines from the sea every year. Sardines eat phytoplankton. Without the fish to eat the plankton, they die off, sink to the bottom and decompose over areas the size of New Jersey, periodically belching up massive eruptions of methane and adding dramatically to global warming, but also resulting in vast areas of the Atlantic Ocean that are so polluted and overfished that they no longer support life larger or more complex than a jellyfish.

At the mouth of the Mississippi River in the Gulf of Mexico, polluted runoff from American farms, factories, and highways create massive "dead zones," thousands of square miles of ocean where normal marine life is obliterated every year. Equally massive garbage patches swirl in a stupefying ballet of plastic trash from urban landscapes and ocean dumping. The greatest tragedy of this litany is that it is one hundred percent preventable.

Figure 15a: *A sea lion with plastic bag in mouth*

Figure 15b: *Coral with plastic bag*

Figure 16: *Ocean dead zone*

And whether we care for JJ or ourselves on this ocean planet, there are many reasons to address these problems now. Numerous cures for various cancers are found in bacteria and proteins harvested from the ocean. Cholera and other human diseases can spread in warm seawater, so as climate change increases ocean temperatures, diseases will surely increase with it. More than half of the seven billion people on earth live near the ocean and depend on it for some part of their food supply—even more of us depend on fertilizer and other byproducts of the fishing industry no matter where we live. The list goes on and on, a list of how interdependent we are with the ocean and all living things in it. At a minimum, JJ is a giant canary in our watery mineshaft. If she cannot get enough food to grow to her natural maturity of seventy years or so, what makes us believe we will fare any better towards our similar lifespan?

Within a day, JJ had scraped the tracking devices from her body and thus shed all evidence of her encounters with humans. The same thing had happened with Gigi, the young gray whale released by SeaWorld decades earlier. SeaWorld and NMFS circulated a flyer to authorities up and down the coast, describing JJ's identifying features, hoping that someone would spot her or, if she washed up dead on a beach, at least her body could be recovered and studied. She had a distinctive scar on her tail and unique markings on her back that might help observers identify her. Days passed, but there was no sighting.

While all eyes strained to catch a glimpse of JJ and learn whether she survived in the wild, what fate awaits her entire species in our century? Will it be the same as the sockeye salmon that once shared the Pacific Northwest waters with gray whales? In 1992, "Larry" became the last sockeye salmon to make it all the way to Idaho's Redfish Lake from the ocean, after swimming a thousand miles upstream in the Columbia and Snake Rivers. NMFS officials, the same ones that determine the fate of stranded whales like JJ, decided that as the last of his kind with such stamina, he should be caught, clubbed to death, and squeezed of his sperm to be used in hatcheries with captive females. His carcass is now mounted on the wall of the office of the construction company that built more than a dozen dams that destroyed the sockeye salmon habitat in the first place, ending the annual migration of tens of thousands of "Larrys"—until there were none. Might JJ live long enough only to become the gray whale equivalent of Larry?

"Whales are very special to me...always have been," said Beverly Hoskinson as we mused about JJ's fate from the beach where we had first found her. "I actually believe we humans have a psychic connection with them and that their well being and ours are connected in the survival of our planet."

A week after JJ's release, Kris told us of a news story from northern California about two gray whale calves that were killed by orcas. We doubted that JJ would have traveled so far in seven days and she was no calf anymore, but it highlighted the challenges she now faced for survival. JJ's sojourn at SeaWorld had already helped her to beat the odds. She was fourteen months at release—as the story of the deaths by orcas reminded us, many causes contribute to the fact that a third of gray whale calves in the wild do not make it to their first birthday.

Days passed and the lack of sightings pushed JJ farther from the front pages of newspapers and minds. Kris and I prepared for the BayKeeper's spring fundraiser called Kelpfest, a whacky beach party that featured finger painting with fish, pirates, steel drums, and a bit of education about protecting the ocean. Peter continued his daily routine of surveying the waters around the Chevron ship terminal for "Doris," a sea lion with fishing nets stuck around her neck, in the hopes that she was still alive and could be freed from the nylon strands that cut deeper into her neck every day. Each of us kept one ear tuned to marine radios and telephones for calls about some new stranded animal to save or egregious polluter to prosecute. Each of us kept one eye peeled from patrol boats and shoreline for signs of a gray whale that might be JJ.

About two weeks after JJ's release, volunteer diver Denise Washko and I loaded our survey and diving gear onto the BayKeeper patrol boat, ready to monitor a kelp restoration site on the southern end of the Santa Monica Bay. Human-caused pollution had contributed to the decimation of the kelp beds in the area, losing vast forests of the giant algae that would otherwise be home to thousands of sea animals. We had perfected a process for replanting kelp and allowing it to take back its former acreage using volunteer divers and donated supplies.

Most days on the kelp project were like this one—7 A.M. at the dock in the foggy morning cold. Lugging heavy gear up and down gangways and securing it in the boat. Tipped cups of lousy coffee on the way to the fuel dock. The smell of toxic benzene fumes, as we topped off the fuel tank, mixed with the acrid odor of rotting sardines and fish guts from the cleaning station nearby. Pelicans diving at the bait box at the end of the fuel dock, eagerly jockeying for a chance to steal a wriggling silvery mouthful. The oppressive smell of layered, aged droppings from gulls, cormorants, pelicans, and sea lions that had all taken turns jousting for a handout.

Denise Washko was a bright, idealistic twenty-seven year old California native whose parents had moved her as a child to Tucson, Arizona, about as far from the ocean as you can get, both physically and emotionally. Her most vivid memories of childhood were not of the desert, but of an annual pilgrimage to San Elijo and Carlsbad State Beaches in northern San Diego County, where her family would spend two weeks camping on the bluffs. These trips cemented her passion for all things ocean and kindled a desire to become a marine biologist. Her studies led her to eco-psychology where she documented the connection between the breakdown of human social systems and the dissolution of natural ecosystems. Now even more motivated to apply her knowledge for the benefit of her beloved oceans, she had moved back to Southern California and volunteered for the BayKeeper's kelp restoration project.

"Like so many Americans, my first glimpse of the ocean world beneath the waves was at SeaWorld in San Diego." Denise reminisced. "I can very fondly recall great excitement about being there but also being very conflicted by seeing the orca whales in captivity and even more concerned about the fact that they were trained like dogs to do tricks. I remember the first time I saw a whale up close in the wild was in the Santa Barbara Channel on a NOAA research vessel. It was a blue whale and it was one of the most memorable experiences of my life. The swells were rather large that day and when the whale would be in the up swell and the boat was down you could see almost the entire body of the whale. It was an amazing experience."

Out on the open sea, we bundled up in our slickers to hold back the cold and the salt spray from the wake made by the fast-moving boat. By the time we reached Rocky Point on Palos Verdes, the peninsula that marks the southern end of the Santa Monica Bay, the sun had burned off most of the morning mist and warmed us considerably. We wrestled with neoprene wetsuits, steel scuba tanks, rubber fins, and foggy glass facemasks, gearing up to make our first survey dive of a new kelp restoration site. On weekends, there were always four or five volunteers to assist but, on a cold weekday in April, I was lucky to have Denise to lend a hand. It was another day at the BayKeeper "office."

With the boat at anchor a few hundred yards from the shore, rising and falling gently on the swells that grew into broad rolling breakers as they approached the shore, we performed the standard inspections of each other's dive gear to be sure everything would function safely on the ocean floor. Denise began peering intently seaward of our location, one palm shading her eyes to cut the glare.

"Is that a whale footprint—there, right there?" she asked, pointing to a patch of calm water about fifty yards from the boat. Before I could see what she meant and make my own guess, the water came to life. A large serpentine body crested the surface and gracefully arched its back, exhaling in a cloud of salty mist that drifted on the breeze in our direction. It was a gray whale, curving distinctively in the pattern of surface-breathe-dive-repeat that suggested it was feeding. We were close enough to see that the waters were murky in the general vicinity of this whale, a telltale sign it was combing the sediments below to strain them for food.

Gray whales migrate north through these waters in April, generally waiting until they reach their Arctic feeding grounds to begin feasting and building up reserves of fat. Adolescents will commonly pause along the route to feed and even adults will take a meal opportunistically when they perceive a bounty in a nearby kelp bed or coastal flat. This whale didn't seem large enough to be a fully-grown adult, but our first glimpse made it hard to know for sure. We did not wait long, however, for clarification.

"Oh…my…god…" Denise cried out, pointing to a spot just a few feet from where the whale had just surfaced. As it arched its back to begin another dive, a diminutive form next to the whale appeared and mimicked the movement. This whale was not alone.

The calf exhaled, barely a squirt of air and water compared to its larger companion, then matched the arching motions and dived in unison with what appeared to be its mother. I stripped off my dive gloves and fumbled with the controls of my underwater camera to be ready the next time this pair surfaced. The larger whale was apparently teaching the calf to feed from the bottom and as we waited for them to resurface, we first saw another plume of beige sediment cover a few square yards of the water, evidence they were scooping and straining on the seafloor. Moments later, the pair surfaced again, almost in the middle of the sediment plume.

"Look, look!" Denise yelled and pointed, making sure I had the camera pointed in the right direction. I clicked away, angry with myself that I didn't have a better camera with a fast automatic shutter. The pair exhaled, almost in perfect unison this time, and disappeared beneath the waves once more in synchronized perfection.

"Did you see that?" I asked. "That whale has no barnacles on its back. There's only one reason a whale that size would have no barnacles—if it was raised in a sterile tank of water and not an open ocean."

"You mean that's JJ?" Denise asked with hesitant hopefulness.

"You look when they come back up. It's not a full-grown adult and it has no barnacles that I could see."

Figure 17: *JJ back in the Santa Monica Bay*

Our excitement at being so close to these whales and watching them feed now became unbearable minutes of waiting for them to reappear so we could test this theory. If it was JJ, what was she doing with a calf? It was obviously not hers. Was there a pod nearby? We had been at anchor for nearly half an hour and neither seen nor heard any other signs of whales in the area. Wanting a closer look, I pulled up the anchor and slowly steered the boat in the general direction of the last plume. I certainly didn't want to scare them away, but we could only confirm the lack of barnacles by getting another close look.

This dive seemed much longer than the last one, but the plume of sediment was suddenly visible on the surface within ten yards of the boat. I shut off the motor and we drifted backwards a few feet before the whales crested again.

Big whoosh. Little whoosh. This time, almost as if they knew we wanted to check them out, the whales rolled to the surface and floated there a minute. I trained binoculars on the pair and marveled at their gentle interaction, almost caressing each other and rolling slightly from one side to the other, the calf playfully slapping its tail and the larger whale nuzzling nose to nose. With a powerful thrust of its tail, the larger one arched well above the waves and began another dive. As the broad flat wingspan of a tail disappeared beneath the wave, the calf following close behind, I could clearly see a distinctive horizontal scar on the upper side of her tail. Right size, no barnacles, distinctive scar. There was no doubt this was JJ.

What explained the calf? It wasn't JJ's, but many whale species are known to put calves in the care of "aunties." JJ had apparently come across another orphan and had adopted it. She was teaching the youngster to swim north, to breathe, to use kelp for protective cover, and to feed from the bottom. The gifts of protection, learning, and life itself that we had given to her, she was now passing on to another.

Sweating in our wetsuits on what had become an unusually warm spring day under a cloudless sky, Denise was talking a mile a minute, questions, observations, commentary. I lowered the binoculars and tears rolled down my cheeks, dried almost at once by the steady morning breeze. I was surprised by such an emotional response, but realized

I was relieved to see JJ alive and apparently adapted to life in the wild, but also deeply moved by the realization that she was now responsible for another young life.

The Chumash people believe that whales and dolphins are humans in another form and at that moment neither of us would argue the kinship we felt with a whale we knew as JJ. We watched for many more minutes as the pair rhythmically surfaced and dove, big whoosh, little whoosh, each time farther north from our position, until our eyes were unable to discern their backs from the waves in the distance and only the puffs of exhaled salt spray punctuated the bright blue sky. At last, we could truly let JJ go, no longer a captive in any sense.

Epilogue

"In this I infer that many things," said Shakespeare, observing a hive of honeybees and their selfless collaboration, "having one consent, they may work apart, but just as many arrows, loosed several ways, come to one mark; as many roads lead to one town; so may a thousand actions, once afoot, end in one purpose, and be all well done to the good of one and all."

E pluribus unum. The profound meaning of JJ's rescue was not just an apparent happy ending, but the message of people from every walk of life coming together in "one consent" and, if we can do it for one of the ocean's creatures, surely we can do so for the ocean itself. Surely we can see the ecosystem on the verge of collapse as clearly as the struggling baby whale in the surf. Surely we can see our connection to that ecosystem—and that saving it from further degradation is actually an act of self-rescue.

We once used whales for oil, then meat, now as circus animals—will we ever just treat them as neighbors? Commercial fishing was probably the world's first truly global, multinational business. In Shakespeare's day, fleets brought back fish to England from North America long before it was a colony of any significance. Whaling soon followed as a great commercial enterprise, especially in the expanding United States, where more than seven hundred of the world's nine hundred whaling ships were based in 1846. In one year, American whalers killed over eight thousand animals for lamp oil, candles, corset stays, perfume ingredients, and a dozen other products. Fortunes were made that would rival today's oil giants.

Also like the modern oil businesses that go to ever-greater lengths to secure the raw materials of their trade, whaling started modestly by harvesting creatures that washed up on the beach or could be caught in shallows. As one resource was exhausted, whalers went to increasing lengths and dangers to keep their profits rolling in. Producers of whale oil, like today's petroleum barons, mocked their competitors and used their political muscle in Washington to protect the industry, until 1859 when a town in Pennsylvania turned petroleum into kerosene that could be burned in lamps and used to lubricate machines instead.

But whaling continued for decades, less for oil and more for meat and other products, virtually exterminating one population after another, including the grays along the California coast and the nursery lagoons of Baja Mexico. In 1975, a little-known non-profit organization ran small boats against Russian whaling ships along the west coast from San Francisco to Vancouver to interfere with any further slaughter of disappearing whale populations. Greenpeace and the modern environmental movement were born and humans tried desperately to reconnect with whales, just as we fumbled for a way to connect with JJ and preserve her life.

So what happened to the key players, the disciples and devils, depending on your perspective, of this particular ecological high drama with one whale in particular?

Denise Washko and her husband Phil moved to Massachusetts, where she continued her work for ocean health with the Coalition for Buzzards Bay, but her life was transformed by giving birth to two children. All she had learned, including the lessons from JJ, were now applied to, and seen through the lens of, her own offspring. She teaches her children about the place they live and their responsibility to it. She tends a large organic vegetable garden and gets really excited about finding new ways to live more "locally."

"I would like to think that JJ is still alive and is spending winters down in the lagoons along Baja California," Denise offers. "I would apologize to her for taking part in the destruction of her habitat and her sources of food. We do what we can to tread a little lighter on this planet and I hope my children will grow up with these practices, as being part of what they do without ever having to think about it. I believe that these small things, done by more people would help a lot more than just the whales. Maybe, in 50 years, many of the changes which are being implemented right now and in the near future will have paid off by then and whales will be getting some breaks."

Like all of us who played a role in the JJ saga, Denise grappled with the conundrum of SeaWorld—are marine theme parks good, because they have the resources to rescue an orphan like JJ, or are they bad, because of the harm imposed on their captives and the family units from which the individual animals are taken? As one of only two people on earth who witnessed what happened to JJ and shared that emotional day of seeing her adopt an orphaned calf of her own, Denise ultimately decided that one was not a reasonable price for the other and will not take her kids to theme parks that display captive whales.

In August of 2007, "Earthman" David Garcia died of liver failure at the age of 63, but much more than a distinguished reporter faded into history that day. David had grown increasingly frustrated with newscasts that featured car chases, gang slayings, and meaningless coverage of beauty tips and sexual fantasies, so he had moved from the Los Angeles NBC network affiliate to work for the local Fox station, where he could cover more environmental stories. When Fox also cut back its environmental reporting, David quit and began producing his own shows for PBS, his website, and anyone who would listen. He packed a van and, with his tireless wife Suzy, drove to Alaska to see what was left of true wilderness. Today, no television news station in America has a reporter dedicated solely to environmental stories.

Peter Wallerstein went on to rescue hundreds of dolphins, sea lions, pelicans, and even helped a few more distressed gray whales. After years of operating solo, he merged with Friends of Animals and began a campaign to build a marine animal rescue center in Marina del Rey, hoping to provide a much-needed "hospital" in the middle of a hundred mile stretch of coastline that had none. He could be seen with a girlfriend now and then, but I suspect they all were lured to him by his rugged good looks, boyish charm, and spotless heart, only to be disillusioned upon discovering that any human in Peter's life would always be a distant second to the animals.

"All I hope is that she's just out there mingling with other gray whales and enjoying her life, swimming free," Peter mused a year after JJ's release. "I hope she stays away from the harpoons...I hope she stays away from the gillnet and the commercial boat traffic...I hope she finds enough food. I mean, out of all of the things that can happen to her, at least I'm so thankful for everybody's efforts...she got a second chance and that's all we could have done...and I'm thankful to SeaWorld. I'm thankful for what they did in their part."

Peter choked a bit on those last words, knowing that SeaWorld had indeed been crucial to one whale's survival, and maybe more, but also knowing that he could never forgive nor forget the cruelty to other whales by SeaWorld, from Taiji to San Diego. He might have accepted that as the price for progress, if SeaWorld or its parent company, Anheuser-Busch, had admitted their part in the slaughter and deception over the years or if they had reformed their parks into marine mammal rehabilitation centers with real education about the plight of these animals. He tried to persuade them by saying they could still make great corporate profits from that approach, as proven by the public appetite for all things JJ. But without something more than a one-time rescue, SeaWorld would not change its business model and Peter would go on campaigning against the captive industry and those who made massive profits from the misery of JJ's kin. Much like the baby whale he helped to rescue, Peter remains a free-spirited work-in-progress.

"I think all our marine life, not just California but worldwide, is still very much in danger and very much threatened, and I think it's going to take a serious fight by lots of people in lots of different levels to protect and preserve what's remaining," he said to a cute girl in a bikini who passed our location on the beach, asking about where she could see dolphins and seals. "I don't feel really good...I hope there are gray whales fifty years from now."

Jim Antrim retired from SeaWorld a few years after JJ's release and kept mostly out of public view. He often spoke of JJ and justifiably took credit for his part in her rescue. As late as August 2008, he shared the recipe for the "baby food" that SeaWorld used to nurse JJ back to her normal robust girth, with activists in Australia who were trying to convince a marine theme park to rescue a whale that had beached nearby. Wildlife officials euthanized that whale, but Antrim's cooperation highlighted the fact that SeaWorld's gamble with JJ had paid off in some ways and, by contrast, how few in his industry were willing to take similar risks.

"The movie is not a fair portrayal of whales in captivity," Antrim told TIME magazine about Free Willy, four years before JJ's rescue. Neither, to this day, is the portrayal by SeaWorld a "fair portrayal" of its captives, displaying what appear to be happy, healthy marine mammals in mutual adoration with their millions of annual visitors. In 2010, SeaWorld was the 22nd most visited attraction on earth and its website brags about conservation efforts, grants, and partnerships with the World Wildlife Fund and Audubon Society, but remains silent on where its star attractions were born, how they were acquired, or how long they are likely to live.

"Human actions and activities can impact all other living organisms on our planet," Antrim points out. "A choice that favors one species frequently is made at the expense of others. In order to make the best decisions possible it is necessary to acquire all the knowledge that can be amassed about the species involved. It is naïve and unrealistic to think we can learn about and understand the animals and plants on earth without bringing them into captive and laboratory environments. Not only does captivity allow us to study certain aspects of these organisms that are impossible to investigate in nature, it also gives humans a proximity to them that creates empathy, concern and an appreciation that would otherwise be unobtainable." Antrim told me that he believes JJ survived.

Despite Peter's efforts and campaigns against the captive marine mammal industry by The Humane Society of the United States and others, SeaWorld hasn't changed the way it capitalizes on the whales and dolphins in its facilities. In 2009, SeaWorld San Diego announced that is was adding a new Las Vegas-style extravaganza, blending circus acrobats with dolphins and whales. The park is adding seven hundred seats in anticipation of bigger crowds and more profits. Dubbed "Blue Horizons," the show premiered at SeaWorld Orlando, where audiences complained that the show featured too many acrobats and not enough dolphins, suggesting that the public hasn't learned much about captive marine mammals since 1998 either.

Rima Heifetz-Loewe continued to rescue animals of all kinds in the Santa Monica Mountains and adjacent shores, volunteering for numerous wildlife organizations. She was a regular at BayKeeper beach cleanups, festivals, lecture nights, and on rainy days when the staff desperately needed help finding the sources of pollution that flush into the bay on stormwater flows.

"The greatest moments in all of my work were when I took the animals back to their homes and set them free," she said after more years and more rescues than can easily be counted. Somehow she also finds time for her own three kids, assorted dogs, and a miniature donkey.

John Heyning of the Natural History Museum died in 2007 of Lou Gehrig's disease at the age of fifty. Like most people, especially those who die young, John's accomplishments were only articulated in his obituary—he added over four thousand specimens to the museum's collection, said to be more than any institution outside the Smithsonian in Washington DC. His flatbed truck had become famous for transporting whales and other ocean creatures on Los Angeles area freeways, but JJ was almost certainly the only one ever to disembark alive. Motorists would often yell at John, "Is it real?" as he sped by.

"Los Angeles is probably the only place in the world where people would see a dead whale on a truck and think it might be fake," Heyning said with his easy chuckle. A colleague described John as "the boy who came home for dinner with a frog in one pocket and a crawfish in the other." As an adult, the "pocket" became that flatbed, without which we would not have been able to get JJ those critical few yards from shore to street.

"I guess I came by my love of the ocean and its creatures naturally and I believe we all had our origins there," Beverly Hoskinson expounded, while thinking back on the decade that had passed for her since JJ's rescue. Her own bout with a life-threatening illness shaped her views of the value of all living things, including animals. "Even my pets played a role in my life and in my recovery. And, in the larger picture, we all need each other and we can all do something to help the other and each of us has a God-given responsibility to do what we can do."

Beverly followed her contributions to JJ's rescue with many more acts of charity. Millions more actually, as the head of the Boeing employee's charity initiatives. In an odd twist of fate, her philanthropy is the reason we know that JJ survived and adopted an orphan of her own. The Santa Monica BayKeeper got that grant, the original reason we were meeting with Beverly on a cold January morning in 1997. It was a grant to start the kelp reforestation project, which a year later is the reason that Denise and I were on the water and able to witness the miracle of JJ's next chapter.

Joe Cordaro and NMFS kept fighting to keep Peter Wallerstein from rescuing marine mammals and birds, but with each success, each animal saved that otherwise would have perished for lack of trained rescuers and equipment in the Santa Monica Bay, with each city that appointed Peter their official rescue coordinator, Joe finally relented. The NMFS website now lists Peter's organization on the official list of approved rescue organizations. Joe was wise to spend many years carefully building the best volunteer rescue network he could—in 2009 he struggled to keep up with record numbers of strandings as climate change, pollution, and other human-caused factors created conditions that resulted in hunger and disease running rampant through colonies of west coast sea lions and other marine mammals. Always the Oz behind the curtain though, he declined to be interviewed for this book.

Kris Haddad and I kept the Santa Monica BayKeeper afloat for several years after JJ's rescue, then handed the growing organization over to a new generation and watched them end pollution to the bay from Los Angeles leaking sewer pipes, from a string of auto wrecking yards, and from Malibu septic tanks. When we were helping JJ, there were a dozen similar Keeper programs around the nation. Today, under the stewardship of Robert F. Kennedy Jr. and more trained environmental professionals than any other non-profit environmental organization on earth, the Waterkeeper Alliance has grown to nearly 200 programs protecting waterways in every part of the globe. The greatest challenge for all environmental activists remains helping people see themselves as part of an ocean planet.

"I can't imagine anything I could do to help the whales in my normal everyday life," a woman told us at KelpFest shortly after JJ's release. "I mean, even when they said to stop buying tuna because tuna fishing killed dolphins, I'm a realist and I think little old me who's not going to buy tuna is not going to help anything. It takes going for much bigger guys than me and my can of tuna now and then."

Kris went on to help small Keeper-like non-profits get started that protect the great redwood forests of California. For several years, I served as the Secretary of the California Environmental Protection Agency, and Kris and I now work together again, this time fighting climate change and the ongoing public ignorance about most environmental topics.

"I wish there was a way to communicate to her that she impacted many lives and through her struggle made people take note of her beauty and importance," Kris said, reminiscing about her own sense of connection to JJ and the profound emotions it left with her. "I think that it is not under the control of the "higher power" as to who or what survives in this world. It's up to each individual human who must look within himself/herself and take responsibility, hopefully act in good conscience."

And what of JJ herself? At least she did not succumb to tribal whaling so far. The Makah took no whales in 1998, but did take a forty-foot female a year later. After exam, it was determined it was not JJ, but was it her mother, Marina? They have taken others since, but none were JJ, based on comparison to the extensive mapping of her scars and skin patterns.

If Marina and JJ successfully navigated the Makah, orcas, the Japanese whalers, the careless boaters, the detritus washing off our urban landscapes, the tourists in their breeding and calving lagoons, and a thousand other slings and arrows of outrageous fortune in the twenty-first century, we know for sure that their fate is quite literally in our hands. Both should live to seventy years, but global warming will have dissipated their food supply long before then. Marina may live to a normal old age, albeit much thinner than normal, but JJ will surely starve to a premature death unless we act now. One whale generation away from extinction, depending on whether we continue to drive a living room on wheels and continue to power our homes with flaming chunks of coal. Or, like the Hopi people, if we evolve to see the world differently.

The Hopi see all things as connected, unlike modern science that takes things apart and studies them in isolation. That's how we are taught in school, seeing animals, ecosystems, water, air, food, sunshine, oceans, rivers, and even the earth itself as oddities to be understood as separate things, at best a fractured mosaic without the perspective of standing back far enough to see how it all works together.

The Hopi people say that one finger cannot lift a pebble. The connected cooperation that we will need to thrive on earth for generations to come will indeed need many fingers acting in concert. Whatever happens to JJ, and those who put their lives on hold for a time to preserve her life, her story illuminates at least one crucial component of a successful path forward—finding some greater good to put before our individual need and doing something in service to that common value.

JJ was the "greater good" for many of us and it can therefore be said, in some small measure at least, she was the whale who saved us.

Figure 18: Baby gray whale breaching

Resource Guide

www.watercolorsthebook.com

Please visit the *Watercolors* website for an updated list of resources and news about the topics covered in this book.

The following organizations are working on ocean conservation, preservation, and protection.

To Get Involved…

- Alaska Whale Foundation: www.alaskawhalefoundation.org
- Alliance for a Living Ocean: www.livingocean.org
- Animal Defenders International: www.adiusa.org
- Atlantic Whale Foundation: www.whalenation.org
- California Coastkeeper: www.cacoastkeeper.org
- Campaign Whale: www.campaign-whale.org
- Coastal Conservation Association: www.joincca.org
- Earthdive: www.earthdive.com
- Earthecho: www.earthecho.org
- Friends of Animals: friendsofanimals.org
- Friends of La Jolla Shores: www.friendsoflajollashores.com
- Friends of the Sea Lion: www.pacificmmc.org
- Grades of Green: www.gradesofgreen.org
- Greenpeace: www.greenpeace.org/usa/en
- Heal the Bay: www.healthebay.org

- Marine Animal Rescue: whalerescueteam.org
- Marine Institute: www.mi.mun.ca/mioceannet
- The Marine Mammal Center: www.tmmc.org
- Monterey Coastkeeper: www.otterproject.org
- National Coalition for Marine Conservation: www.savethefish.org
- National Fish and Wildlife Foundation: www.nfwf.org
- Ocean Alliance: www.oceanalliance.org
- Ocean Futures Society: www.oceanfutures.org
- Ocean Net: www.oceannet.ca
- Ocean Research and Conservation Association: www.oceanrecon.org
- Ocean Revolution: www.oceanrevolution.org
- Oceana: na.oceana.org
- Orange County Coastkeeper: www.coastkeeper.org
- Pacific Marine Mammal Center: www.pacificmmc.org
- Pacific Whale Foundation www.pacificwhale.org/
- Peconic Baykeeper: www.peconicbaykeeper.org
- Reef Relief: www.reefrelief.org
- San Diego Coastkeeper: www.sdcoastkeeper.org
- San Francisco Baykeeper: baykeeper.org
- San Luis Obispo Coastkeeper: www.epicenteronline.org
- Santa Monica Baykeeper: www.smbaykeeper.org
- Save-a-Turtle: www.save-a-turtle.org
- Save our Seas: www.saveourseas.org
- Save the Waves Coalition: www.savethewaves.org
- Save the Whales: www.savethewhales.org
- Sea Shepherd Conservation Society: www.seashepherd.org
- Sea Watch Foundation: www.seawatchfoundation.org.uk
- Seaturtle.org: www.seaturtle.org

- Shark Alliance: www.sharkalliance.org
- Surfers Environmental Alliance: www.seasurfer.org
- Surfrider Foundation USA: www.surfrider.org
- Waterkeeper Alliance: www.waterkeeper.org (Note: There are over 200 operating Waterkeeper organizations. To find a Waterkeeper near you, please visit www.waterkeeper.org/ht/d/OrgDir/pid/210)
- WildAid: www.wildaid.org
- Whales Alive: www.whalesalive.org.au
- Whale and Dolphin Conservation Society: www.wdcs.org
- Whale Rescue Team: whalerescueteam.org
- Whale Tail License Plate: www.coastal.ca.gov/publiced/plate/platefaq.html

To Learn More…

- Alaska Whale Foundation: www.alaskawhalefoundation.org
- Algalita Marine Research Foundation: www.algalita.org/index.php
- The American Shore and Beach Preservation Association: www.asbpa.org
- Blue Ocean Institute: www.blueocean.org/home
- Changing Seas: changingseas.tv
- Clean Ocean Foundation: www.cleanocean.org
- Coral Reef Alliance: www.coral.org
- Coral Reef Research Institute: www.reef.edu.au/CRRI
- Earth Island Institute: www.earthisland.org
- Eco-Warrior: ecosurfwarrior.blogspot.com
- The Foundation for Center for Research for Whales: www.researchwhales.com
- International Ocean Institute: www.ioinst.org
- Marine Bio:

marinebio.org/oceans/conservation/organizations.asp

- Marine Conservation Biology Institute: www.mcbi.org
- Marine Fish Conservation Network: www.conservefish.org
- Monterey Bay Aquarium Research Institute: www.mbari.org
- National Coral Reef Institute: www.nova.edu/ncri
- North Gulf Oceanic Society: www.whalesalaska.org
- The Ocean Conservancy: www.oceanconservancy.org
- Open Oceans: openoceans.com
- Protect Planet Ocean: www.protectplanetocean.org
- Scripps Institution of Oceanography: sio.ucsd.edu
- Seal Conservation Society: www.pinnipeds.org
- Seas at Risk: www.seas-at-risk.org
- The Whale Trust: www.whaletrust.org/whales/whale_conservation.shtml
- Whalenet: whale.wheelock.edu

To See Whales in Person...

- Baja Jones Adventures: www.greywhale.com/whale_watching_in_baja.htm
- Monterey Bay Whale Watch Trips: www.montereybaywhalewatch.com/trips.htm
- The Whale Museum: www.whalemuseum.org/programs/graywhale/grayproj.html

Endnotes

Chapter 1

BBC. 2007. Planet Earth – Deep Ocean. London: BBC-Warner Video

Brower, Kenneth. 2005. Freeing Keiko. New York: Gotham Books

Coerr, Eleanor & Evans, Dr. William E. 1980. Gigi – A Baby Whale Borrowed for Science and Returned to the Sea. New York: Putnam & Sons.

Dando, Marc & Burchett, Michael & Waller, Geoffrey. 1996. SeaLife – A Complete Guide to the Marine Environment. Washington, DC: Smithsonian Institution Press

Dedina, Serge. 2000. Saving the Gray Whale. Tucson: University of Arizona Press

Dolan, Eric Jay. 2008. Leviathan – The History of Whaling in America. New York: WW Norton

Ingmanson, Dale E. & Wallace, William J. 1989. Oceanography: An Introduction. Belmont: Wadsworth Publishing Co.

KQED & Ocean Futures Society. 2006. Jean-Michel Cousteau Ocean Adventures. Washington, DC: PBS Home Video

Mellville, Herman. 2003. Moby-Dick or, The Whale. New York: Penguin Books

Montgomery, David. 2003. King of Fish – The Thousand Year Run of Salmon. Boulder: Westview Press

Oceanic Society. 1989. Field Guide to the Gray Whale. Seattle: Sasquatch Books

Peterson, Brenda & Hogan, Linda. 2002. Sightings: The Gray Whales' Mysterious Journey. Washington, DC: National Geographic

Rice, Dale W. & Wolman, Allen A. 1971. The Life History and Ecology of the Gray Whale (Eschrichtius robustus). Seattle: American Society of Mammologists

SeaWorld Accounts of JJ Captivity, Aquatic Mammals 2001, 27.3

SlingShot Entertainment. 1997. Whales – An Unforgettable Journey. Burbank: DVD

Thelander, Carl G. & Crabtree, Margo. 1994. Life on the Edge. Santa Cruz: BioSystems Analysis, Inc

Wolpert, Tom. 1990. Whales for Kids. Minocqua: NorthWord Press

Chapter 2

Allsopp, Michele; Page, Richard, Johnston, Paul; Santillo, David, Oceans in Peril (Washington, DC: Worldwatch Institute, September 2007)

BBC. 2007. Planet Earth – Deep Ocean. London: BBC-Warner Video

Brandon, Jeffrey; Rokop, Frank J. 1985. Life Between the Tides. San Diego, CA: American Southwest Publishing Co.

Brower, Kenneth. 2005. Freeing Keiko. New York: Gotham Books

Carwardine, Mark; Hoyt, Erich; Fordyce, R. Ewan; Gill, Peter. 1998. Whales, Dolphins, & Porpoises. Sydney: The Nature Company

Clark, RB. 1992. Marine Pollution. Oxford: Clarendon Press.

Connor, Judith; Baxter, Charles. 1989. Kelp Forests. Monterey, CA: Monterey Bay Aquarium Publications.

Dando, Marc & Burchett, Michael & Waller, Geoffrey. 1996. SeaLife – A Complete Guide to the Marine Environment. Washington, DC: Smithsonian Institution Press

Dedina, Serge. 2000. Saving the Gray Whale. Tucson: University of Arizona Press

Ingmanson, Dale E. & Wallace, William J. 1989. Oceanography: An Introduction. Belmont: Wadsworth Publishing Co.

KQED & Ocean Futures Society. 2006. Jean-Michel Cousteau Ocean Adventures. Washington, DC: PBS Home Video

Montgomery, David. 2003. King of Fish – The Thousand Year Run of Salmon. Boulder: Westview Press

Ocean (Wikipedia, March 2009)

Oceanic Society. 1989. Field Guide to the Gray Whale. Seattle: Sasquatch Books

Panetta, Leon (Chair), America's Living Oceans (Washington, DC: Pew Oceans Commission, May 2003)

Personal communication, Phillip J. Clapham, Ph.D. Large Whale Biology Program, Northeast Fisheries Science Center, Woods Hole, MA,

April 19, 2000

Rice, Dale W. & Wolman, Allen A. 1971. The Life History and Ecology of the Gray Whale (Eschrichtius robustus). Seattle: American Society of Mammologists

Russell, Dick. 2001. Eye of the Whale. Washington, DC: Island Press

Scientists Find a Microbe Haven at Ocean's Surface. New York Times, July 28, 2009

Thelander, Carl G. & Crabtree, Margo. 1994. Life on the Edge. Santa Cruz: BioSystems Analysis, Inc

SlingShot Entertainment. 1997. Whales – An Unforgettable Journey. Burbank: DVD

Suzuki, David. 1997. The Sacred Balance. Vancouver: Greystone Books.

Chapter 3

A Whale of a Business, FRONTLINE, http://www.pbs.org/wgbh/pages/frontline/shows/whales/etc/script.html, November 11, 1997

Brower, Kenneth. 2005. Freeing Keiko. New York: Gotham Books

Captive Marine Mammals – Information Packet. The Humane Society of the United States, Washington, DC: 1996

Causes of Death – Captive Marine Mammals, South Florida Sun-Sentinel, March 2009

Clarke, Chris. Frontline interview with Susan Davis, author of Spectacular Nature. www.frontline.org: 1997

Coerr, Eleanor & Evans, Dr. William E. 1980. Gigi – A Baby Whale Borrowed for Science and Returned to the Sea. New York: Putnam & Sons.

Davis, Susan G. 1997. Spectacular Nature. Berkeley: University of California Press

Dedina, Serge. 2000. Saving the Gray Whale. Tucson: University of Arizona Press

Hemmi, Sakae. Driven By Demand. (Chippenham, Wiltshire, UK: Whale and Dolphin Conservation Society: 2006)

Oceanic Society. 1989. Field Guide to the Gray Whale. Seattle: Sasquatch Books

Personal communication. Kristina Haddad, Programs Director, Santa Monica BayKeeper, Marina del Rey, CA. August 25, 2008

Personal communication, Peter Wallerstein, President, Whale Rescue Team, Marina del Rey, CA. November 20, 2002

Personal communication, Rima Heifetz-Loewe, volunteer, Santa Monica BayKeeper, Marina del Rey, CA. December 11, 2008

Peterson, Brenda & Hogan, Linda. 2002. Sightings: The Gray Whales' Mysterious Journey. Washington, DC: National Geographic

Rice, Dale W. & Wolman, Allen A. 1971. The Life History and Ecology of the Gray Whale (Eschrichtius robustus). Seattle: American Society of Mammologists

Rose, Naomi A. Captive Cetaceans: The Science Behind the Ethics. (Presented at the European Cetacean Society 18th Annual Conference, Kolmården, Sweden Humane Society of the United States: 2004)

Rose, Naomi A. The Case Against Marine Mammals in Captivity (Washington, DC, The Human Society of the United States: 1999)

Russell, Dick. 2001. Eye of the Whale. Washington, DC: Island Press

Small, Robert J. & DeMaster, Douglas P. Survival of Five Species of Captive Marine Mammals (Seattle, WA: National Marine Mammal Laboratory; Alaska Fisheries Science Center; National Marine Fisheries Service: 1995)

Smolker, Rachel. 2002. To Touch a Wild Dolphin. New York: Random House

Williams, Vanessa. Dying to Entertain You (Chippenham, Wiltshire, UK: Whale and Dolphin Conservation Society: 2001)

Woodley, Thomas H. & Hannah, Janice L. & Lavigne, David M. Comparison of survival rates for wild vs captive whales/ dolphins (Guelph, Ontario: International Marine Mammal Association. 1997)

Chapter 4

Brower, Kenneth. 2005. Freeing Keiko. New York: Gotham Books

Journey North. Annenberg Media. 2000. www.learner.org/ jnorth/gwhale

Mellville, Herman. 2003. Moby-Dick or, The Whale. New York: Penguin Books

Personal communication. Kristina Haddad, Programs Director, Santa Monica BayKeeper, Marina del Rey, CA. August 25, 2008

Personal communication, Peter Wallerstein, President, Whale Rescue Team, Marina del Rey, CA. November 20, 2002

Personal communication, Rima Heifetz-Loewe, volunteer, Santa Monica BayKeeper, Marina del Rey, CA. December 11, 2008

Peterson, Brenda & Hogan, Linda. 2002. Sightings: The Gray Whales' Mysterious Journey. Washington, DC: National Geographic

Russell, Dick. 2001. Eye of the Whale. Washington, DC: Island Press

Chapter 5

A Fall From Freedom, Earth Views Productions, 1998.

Allsopp, Michele; Page, Richard, Johnston, Paul; Santillo, David, Oceans in Peril (Washington, DC: Worldwatch Institute, September 2007)

Bad News from the Blubber, Living on Earth, February 15, 2008

Captive Marine Mammals – Information Packet. The Humane Society of the United States, Washington, DC: 1996

Coerr, Eleanor & Evans, Dr. William E. 1980. Gigi – A Baby Whale Borrowed for Science and Returned to the Sea. New York: Putnam & Sons.

Could cat waste be killing sea otters? Journal of the American Veterinary Medical Association, March 15, 2003

Dolphin Hunt Sags Amid Mercury Fears, The Guardian, January 31, 2008

He sounds alarm on polluted oceans, Boston Globe, January 7, 2008

Ingmanson, Dale E. & Wallace, William J. 1989. Oceanography: An Introduction. Belmont: Wadsworth Publishing Co.

Mellville, Herman. 2003. Moby-Dick or, The Whale. New York: Penguin Books

National Geographic (video). Whales in Crisis. 2006

Niemann, Greg. 2002. Baja Legends: The Historic Characters, Events, and Locations That Put Baja CA on the Map. El Cajon: Sunbelt Publications

Personal communication. Kristina Haddad, Programs Director, Santa Monica BayKeeper, Marina del Rey, CA. August 25, 2008

Personal communication, Peter Wallerstein, President, Whale Rescue Team, Marina del Rey, CA. November 20, 2002

Personal communication, Rima Heifetz-Loewe, volunteer, Santa Monica BayKeeper, Marina del Rey, CA. December 11, 2008

Peterson, Brenda & Hogan, Linda. 2002. Sightings: The Gray Whales' Mysterious Journey. Washington, DC: National Geographic

Russell, Dick. 2001. Eye of the Whale. Washington, DC: Island Press

SeaWorld Accounts of JJ Captivity, Aquatic Mammals 2001, 27.3

Small, R. and D. DeMaster (1995b). Acclimation to captivity: a quantitive estimate based on survival of bottlenose dolphins and California sea lions. Marine Mammal Science, Vol. 11:4, p. 510-519.

Smolker, Rachel. 2002. To Touch a Wild Dolphin. New York: Random House

Star Trek IV: The Voyage Home, Paramount Pictures 1986

The JJ Story. Seaworld. 1998. accessed 2009 at http://www.you-tube.com/watch?v=MXvlYY11B9g

Thelander, Carl G. & Crabtree, Margo. 1994. Life on the Edge. Santa Cruz: BioSystems Analysis, Inc

Thompson, Doug. 2006. Whales – Touching the Mystery. Troutdale: NewSage Press

Woodley, Thomas H. & Hannah, Janice L. & Lavigne, David M. Comparison of survival rates for wild vs captive whales/dolphins (Guelph, Ontario: International Marine Mammal Association. 1997)

Chapter 6

Arnold, Catherine and Hewett, Richard. 1999. Baby Whale Rescue – The True Story of JJ. Mahwah: Bridgewater Books

Brower, Kenneth. 2005. Freeing Keiko. New York: Gotham Books

Coerr, Eleanor & Evans, Dr. William E. 1980. Gigi – A Baby Whale Borrowed for Science and Returned to the Sea. New York: Putnam & Sons.

Peterson, Brenda & Hogan, Linda. 2002. Sightings: The Gray Whales' Mysterious Journey. Washington, DC: National Geographic

Rice, Dale W. & Wolman, Allen A. 1971. The Life History and Ecology of the Gray Whale (Eschrichtius robustus). Seattle: American Society of Mammologists

Personal communication, Beverly Hoskinson, Director, Boeing Employees Community Fund, Los Angeles, CA October 16, 2008

Personal communication. Jim Antrim, Vice President of Zoological Operations, SeaWorld San Diego (retired) by phone July 29, 2009

Personal communication. Kristina Haddad, Programs Director, Santa Monica BayKeeper, Marina del Rey, CA. August 25, 2008

Personal communication, Peter Wallerstein, President, Whale Rescue Team, Marina del Rey, CA. November 20, 2002

Personal communication, Rima Heifetz-Loewe, volunteer, Santa Monica BayKeeper, Marina del Rey, CA. December 11, 2008

Russell, Dick. 2001. Eye of the Whale. Washington, DC: Island Press

SeaWorld accounts and scientific papers of JJ's captivity, Aquatic Mammals 2001, 27.3

The JJ Story. Seaworld 1998 accessed July 2009 at http://www.youtube.com/watch?v=MXvlYY11B9g and at http://www.seaworld.org/animal-info/gray-whale/movies-main.htm

Top ten facts whalers don't want you to know. World Society for the Protection of Animals. http://www.wspa-international.org viewed August 1, 2009

Tribal Group Kills Whale Off Washington, New York Times, September 11, 2007

Chapter 7

A giant of the sea finds slimmer pickings, Los Angeles Times, July 6, 2007

Allsopp, Michele; Page, Richard, Johnston, Paul; Santillo, David, Oceans in Peril (Washington, DC: Worldwatch Institute, September 2007)

Arnold, Catherine and Hewett, Richard. 1999. Baby Whale Rescue – The True Story of JJ. Mahwah: Bridgewater Books

Brower, Kenneth. 2005. Freeing Keiko. New York: Gotham Books

Coerr, Eleanor & Evans, Dr. William E. 1980. Gigi – A Baby Whale Borrowed for Science and Returned to the Sea. New York: Putnam & Sons.

Dolan, Eric Jay. 2008. Leviathan – The History of Whaling in America. New York: WW Norton

Gray whale recovery called incorrect. Los Angeles Times, September 11, 2007

KQED & Ocean Futures Society. 2006. Jean-Michel Cousteau Ocean Adventures. Washington, DC: PBS Home Video

Mellville, Herman. 2003. Moby-Dick or, The Whale. New York: Penguin Books

Neptune's Medicine Chest. Los Angeles Times, May 18, 2006

Ocean Health and Human Health. Environmental Health Perspectives, April 2004 (Volume 112, Number 5)

On a Remote Path to Cures, New York Times, January 1, 2008

Personal communication, Beverly Hoskinson, Director, Boeing Employees Community Fund, Los Angeles, CA October 16, 2008

Personal communication, Denise Washko, volunteer, Santa Monica BayKeeper, Marina del Rey, CA. December 10, 2008

Personal communication. Kristina Haddad, Programs Director, Santa Monica BayKeeper, Marina del Rey, CA. August 25, 2008

Personal communication, Peter Wallerstein, President, Whale Rescue Team, Marina del Rey, CA. November 20, 2002

Personal communication, Rima Heifetz-Loewe, volunteer, Santa Monica BayKeeper, Marina del Rey, CA. December 11, 2008

Peterson, Brenda & Hogan, Linda. 2002. Sightings: The Gray Whales' Mysterious Journey. Washington, DC: National Geographic

Rice, Dale W. & Wolman, Allen A. 1971. The Life History and

Ecology of the Gray Whale (Eschrichtius robustus). Seattle: American Society of Mammologists

Scientists fear 'tipping point' in Pacific Ocean. Seattle Post-Intelligencer, February 14, 2008

SeaWorld Accounts of JJ Captivity, Aquatic Mammals 2001, 27.3

Star Trek IV: The Voyage Home, Paramount Pictures 1986

Suzuki, David. 1997. The Sacred Balance. Vancouver: Greystone Books

The Next Ocean. Science News Online, Week of March 15, 2008 (Vol. 173, No. 11)

They Used to Say Whale Oil Was Indispensable, Too. New York Times. August 3, 2008

Tribal Group Kills Whale Off Washington, New York Times, September 11, 2007

Epilogue

A sad goodbye. Sea Shepherd Magazine. August 22, 2008

Dolan, Eric Jay. 2008. Leviathan – The History of Whaling in America. New York: WW Norton

John Heyning, leading marine biologist with L.A. museum, dead at 50. San Diego Union Tribune, February 24, 2007

Personal communication, Beverly Hoskinson, Director, Boeing Employees Community Fund, Los Angeles, CA October 16, 2008

Personal communication, Denise Washko, volunteer, Santa Monica BayKeeper, Marina del Rey, CA. December 10, 2008

Personal communication. Kristina Haddad, Programs Director, Santa Monica BayKeeper, Marina del Rey, CA. August 25, 2008

Personal communication, Peter Wallerstein, President, Whale Rescue Team, Marina del Rey, CA. November 20, 2002

Personal communication, Rima Heifetz-Loewe, volunteer, Santa Monica BayKeeper, Marina del Rey, CA. December 11, 2008

Prince of Whales. TIME Magazine, July 19, 1993

Sea lions are flooding into Bay Area rescue centers. Los Angeles Times, July 15, 2009

SeaWorld San Diego combines acrobats and dolphins for new 'Blue Horizons' show, Los Angeles Times, August 5, 2009

Shakespeare, William. Henry V, Act 1 Scene 2

Suzuki, David. 1997. The Sacred Balance. Vancouver: Greystone Books

The JJ Story. Seaworld 1998 accessed July 1, 2009 at http://www.youtube.com/watch?v=MXvlYY11B9g

They Used to Say Whale Oil Was Indispensable, Too. New York Times. August 3, 2008

Theme Park Attendance. Amusement Business 2009 (as reported on CoasterGrotto.com)

About the Author

Terry Tamminen served as the Secretary of the California Environmental Protection Agency for Governor Schwarzenegger and is currently the President of Seventh Generation Advisors and an Operating Advisor to Pegasus Capital Advisors. From his youth in Australia to career experiences in Europe, Africa, China and across the United States, Terry has developed expertise in business, farming, education, non-profit, the environment, the arts, and government.

A United States Coast Guard-licensed ship captain, Terry has long been drawn to the undersea world, starting in the 1960s with a family-run tropical fish breeding business in Australia and continuing with studies on conch depletion in the Bahamas, manatee populations in Florida coastal waters, and mariculture in the Gulf States with Texas A&M University.

On land, Terry managed the largest sheep ranch east of the Mississippi, assisting the University of Minnesota in developing new methods of livestock disease control. Terry also managed a multi-million dollar real estate company, owned a successful recreational services business, and assisted the West African nation of Nigeria with the creation of their first solid waste recycling program.

In 1993, Terry founded the Santa Monica BayKeeper and co-founded additional Waterkeeper programs in five California watersheds. He later served as the Executive Director of the Environment Now Foundation in Santa Monica, CA, and co-founded the Frank G. Wells Environmental Law Clinic at the School of Law, University of California Los Angeles.

In the summer of 2003, Terry helped Arnold Schwarzenegger win the historic recall election and become Governor of California. He was appointed as the Secretary of the California Environmental Protection Agency in November 2003 and was later appointed Cabinet Secretary, the Chief Policy Advisor to the Governor. During his service in state government, Terry was the architect of many groundbreaking sustainability policies, including California's landmark Global Warming Solutions Act of 2006, the Hydrogen Highway Network, and the Million Solar Roofs initiative.

Terry left state government in late 2006 in order to help other states and world governments adopt clean energy and sustainability policies based on California's successes. In February 2007, he founded the non-profit organization Seventh Generation Advisors (SGA). SGA's strategy is to create a "bottom up" approach, rather than waiting for policy from the top. This strategic approach has proven successful, and since 2007, Terry and SGA convinced many states and provinces to copy California policies and other "best practices" on clean energy and climate policy.

In 2007 he was also named the Cullman Senior Fellow for climate policy at the New America Foundation and was appointed as an Operating Advisor to Pegasus Capital Advisors, a private equity fund that provides capital to middle market companies across a wide variety of industries specializing in resource efficiency and sustainable technologies.

In 2011 Terry was appointed as the R20 Founding Chair's Strategic Advisor. The R20 Regions of Climate Action, created in 2010 by Governor Arnold Schwarzenegger and other sub-national leaders, is a new public-private partnership, bringing together sub-national governments; businesses; financial markets; NGOs; and academia to implement measurable, large-scale, low-carbon and climate resilient economic development projects that can simultaneously solve the climate crisis and build a sustainable global economy. As the Founding Chair's Strategic Advisor, Terry is advising the R20 on policy and helping with the design and implementation of climate resilient economic development projects.

An accomplished author, Terry's book, *Cracking the Carbon Code: The Keys to Sustainable Profits in the New Economy* (Palgrave), shows how to find the low carbon products and services that save money, get ahead of regulations, and preserve resources for generations to come. Terry's previous book, *Lives Per Gallon: The True Cost of Our Oil Addiction* (Island Press), is a timely examination of our dependence on oil and a strategy to evolve to more sustainable energy sources. He has also authored a series of best-selling "Ultimate Guides" to pools and spas (McGraw-Hill) and several theatrical works on the life of William Shakespeare. Terry is an avid airplane and helicopter pilot and speaks German, Dutch and Spanish.

Terry was one of six finalists for the 2011 Zayed Future Energy Prize, which offers $2.2 million of awards in the category of clean, sustainable energy recognizing individuals, non-profits, and companies that are doing the most to commercialize and distribute renewable energy to replace fossil fuels and cut pollution. Terry Tamminen was named Vanity Fair's May 2007 Environmental Hero and in *Time Magazine's* 2007 Earthday edition, he was featured in the "51 Things We Can Do" section. In 2008, *The Guardian* ranked Terry No. 1 in its "Top 50 People Who Can Save the Planet." In 2009, Tamminen was named an "Eco Baron" in Pulitzer Prize-winning journalist Edward Humes's book, *Eco Barons: The Dreamers, Schemers, and Millionaires Who Are Saving Our Planet.*